"An excellent strategic and tactical career guide for training and development professionals to use in navigating today's turbulent and ever-changing world of work. Provides both the "big picture" context for changes taking place in organizations and the global economy today, and a wealth of practical tips and advice on how to navigate this ever-shifting terrain successfully. A highly readable and informative book for anyone who wants to capitalize on change to move ahead in their T&D career!"

Rick Koonce
Managing Principal and Senior Executive Coach
The Huntington Northstar Group LLC

"This book is a search engine for success! Every T&D professional's career will benefit from Williams and Reitman's thorough compilation of trends, in-demand competencies, and insightful ideas."

Susan Whitcomb, PCC
CEO of The Academies for coach certification training
author of 7 career books, including *Résumé Magic and Interview Magic*

"Whenever I want to learn the latest and the greatest, I look to training industry professionals, individuals I personally know and professionally follow. I want to know what they know, how they use that knowledge, and *why* it's important for me to know. In *Career Moves*, my colleague, Caitlin Williams, along with Annabelle Reitman, has written a book that tells me precisely what I want to know about T&D—today, tomorrow, and in the future. Williams and Reitman provide a wonderful road map for professional career success for all T&D professionals. Thank you for this wonderful resource!"

Wendy Enelow
Founder and Executive Director, Career Thought Leaders Consortium
and the Resume Writing Academy

"Williams and Reitman have fashioned a comprehensive, highly accessible 'round up' of pragmatic and strategic career advice suitable for all professional audiences. Anchored with the foundation of the training and development competencies, they punctuate all the core elements requisite to discovering, securing and celebrating work that truly matters, wherever you are in this complex world of choice and change. Career development professionals should find this especially useful in navigating their own as well as their clients' work paths, complemented by the rich global overlays of culture and innovation."

Heather F. Turnbull, CMF
Global President,
Association of Career Professionals International (ACP International)

CAREER MOVES

Be Strategic About Your Future

Caitlin Williams and Annabelle Reitman

ASTD Press is an internationally renowned source of insightful and practical information on workplace learning, performance, and professional development.

ASTD Press
1640 King Street Box 1443
Alexandria, VA 22313-1443 USA

Ordering information: Books published by ASTD Press can be purchased by visiting ASTD's website at store.astd.org or by calling 800.628.2783 or 703.683.8100.

Library of Congress Control Number: 2013946169
ISBN-10: 1-56286-868-3
ISBN-13: 978-1-56286-868-0
e-ISBN: 978-1-60728-749-0

ASTD Press Editorial Staff:
Director: Glenn Saltzman
Manager, ASTD Press: Ashley McDonald
Community Managers, Career Development: Jennifer Homer and Phaedra Brotherton
Senior Associate Editor: Heidi Smith
Editorial Assistant: Sarah Cough
Text and Cover Design: Lon Levy and Ana Foreman
Printed by: Versa Press, East Peoria, IL
www.versapress.com

Table of Contents

Dedication

I dedicate this book to Stan, Helen, Hannah, and Ray for their generosity of spirit and for encouraging and modeling each and every day what it means to truly embrace the full range of life's possibilities.

—Caitlin Williams

To Sylvia Benatti—my friend, collaborator, and colleague. Thanks for all your support, active listening, and just being there throughout this revision. And to Rachael, who thinks it's wonderful having a mother in the 4th phase (and most creative one) of her career.

—Annabelle Reitman

Preface

Welcome to the 3rd edition of *Career Moves: Be Strategic About Your Future*! When we wrote the first edition in 2001, few books were available that spoke directly to professionals in the training and development field who sought career guidance on how to enter the field, identify opportunities within it, and move ahead. In 2006, when we wrote the 2nd edition, information that specifically addressed careers within training and development was still scarce. Today that situation hasn't changed very much; however, the way T&D professionals go about their work continues to change as the workforce and workplace demands have transformed our roles significantly. All these changes require us to be savvier than ever about how to help organizations make important changes, how to help employees continue to contribute their best, and how to consider our own career development and job search strategies.

Therefore, this latest edition of *Career Moves* was written to keep people informed about the latest developments and updates in the training and development field. A revised ASTD Competency Model was published earlier this year that includes new ways of describing and defining the profession, and it offers guidance on the key competencies needed to succeed as a training and development professional today. This enhanced and revised edition of *Career Moves* is meant to capture these significant changes and provide information and tools enabling practical application to the shape and direction of one's T&D career.

As the workplace itself continues to evolve at breathtaking speed, a review and discussion of the latest trends, issues, challenges, and opportunities that are a part of today's (and tomorrow's) work setting are critical, especially when determining how best to respond to the needs of workers who are constantly facing new demands to learn and improve their performance.

What it takes to be successful in our profession has changed, and will continue to do so—and that is one of the central reasons for this 3rd edition of *Career Moves: Be Strategic About Your Future*. In summary, this book offers you a look at the latest workplace and workforce trends and issues and how they can affect the training and development field and your own career. This book also features the newly revised ASTD Competency Model and describes how you can use it as a tool and a guide to prepare you for work in the field. The book also presents ideas and exercises for ongoing professional development goals to stay on the cutting edge and contribute your best—as well as ensure your own employability in the years ahead.

In all three editions, we took a unique approach in developing this book by focusing on the topics that each of us is most passionate about and then writing about them in the two distinct sections of the book. Section I, written by Caitlin, provides critical information affecting training professionals. Chapter 1 details eight trends, providing websites, videos, and podcasts for expanding the depth of your understanding. Since it has a lot of information, you could either read straight through, or focus on specific trends, returning to reference and increase the contexts of the trends. Chapter 2 introduces the 2013 ASTD Competency Model and explains how it applies to T&D professionals. In chapter 3, you will learn how to set yourself apart in your field. Chapter 4 continues with how to use all of the opportunities available to you, introducing some examples of T&D professionals in various stages of career development. The profiles of these four training and development professionals continue throughout the remainder of the book to help you see how they develop their own strategy for going forward.

Annabelle wrote Section II of this book, which stresses the how and why of the career management process and provides a discussion of volunteer and mentoring activities as alternative professional growth experiences. In addition, chapter 9, "Marketing Your Professional Strengths," expanded the section about using the Internet to market and brand yourself, with a new section on social media tools, and introduced the concept of "telling your professional story." Chapter 10 stresses the essentials of branding. There is more enhanced content at the end of chapters 5-10, with Chapter Highlights that list a series of questions regarding what you learned and how that information can be applied to career goals and professional dreams.

Our objectives in writing this book were to:

- Describe the evolving T&D field and its impact on professionals choosing to work and grow in this area.

- Provide practical tools and resources useful in planning for further enhancement and progression in the field.

- Help you understand the importance of taking control of your professional journey, including its movements, stops, and final destination.

If you've already read the previous editions of *Career Moves* and you've returned to see what's new, welcome back! We're delighted you're here, and we know you'll appreciate the latest information and guidance that we'll be sharing with you.

If you are new to the profession of training, performance improvement, coaching, or any other related area of human resource development, you'll find valuable information on recent thinking in the field, together with the latest trends, important key competencies, and the tools and exercises that will help you succeed in your career.

We hope you're as energized by reading this book as we were in writing it. It truly still is (and will remain so) an exciting time to be in this field, where the ways we can make a difference, the areas of expertise we can share, and the roles we can play have never been so varied. In the T&D field, all of our work has never been more accepted and acknowledged. So let's get started—turn the page and we'll help you perform at your very best!

—Annabelle Reitman and Caitlin Williams
September 2013

Overview of Workplace Trends, T&D Competencies, and Your Opportunities

Introduction

Thomas Friedman and Michael Mandelbaum, authors of *That Used to Be Us: How America Fell Behind in the World It Invented and How We Can Come Back,* have a message for us: "Average is officially over" (2011). Average isn't enough for nations, corporations, leaders, or workers. And it isn't enough for training and development professionals—those charged with bringing out the best qualities, finest skills, and enduring commitments of workers and organizations.

That's why "average" is not what this book is about. *Career Moves* is your road map to learning, understanding, and then putting to use—for yourself and those you serve—the latest workplace trends, competencies, critical areas of expertise, and professional opportunities that will position you for success in our volatile and ever-changing workplace.

Join us as we guide you on the best routes to take, the most relevant road signs to pay attention to, and the best direction to steer toward so you can experience a series of successful career moves. Section I of this book can be a valuable resource, whether you are an aspiring undergrad; a graduate student with some specialized focus; a newly hired trainer beginning your first job; a mid-career professional questioning your next career move; or an executive in our field. As you read through the chapters that follow, you'll learn about emerging trends, critical competencies, and areas of expertise, as well as important information on how to distinguish yourself in your field. As you review this section, continue to ask yourself what all this information means for your own career development. You may have read a particular fact about learning, training, or globalization before. But, even if you have, how much time have you taken to reflect on that fact or particular trend's importance and relevance for your own career choices and direction?

As a professional in the training and development field, you probably spend a good amount of your time helping others to grow and succeed. Consider this an opportunity to take some time for your own growth and development.

—Caitlin Williams

Chapter 1

Leverage the Latest Workplace & Workforce Trends

An Overview of Emerging Trends and What They Mean for T&D Professionals

Most of us have grown accustomed to seeing articles, blogs, and magazine cover stories about emerging trends everywhere and on every possible topic. There are trends on the latest fashion styles, home ownership options, social networking sites— even trends on the most popular names for newborns. We quickly scan these articles, listen to the 30-second news item, or click on YouTube to see someone showing off the most outrageous trend in teen hairstyles in Singapore or Seattle. But beyond these snapshots and sound bites, information on these trends doesn't really rock our world. Why? Because while these trends may be amusing or interesting in the moment, they don't have much to do with our own lives.

The trends you'll read about in this chapter are different—and here's why. These trends are focused on workplace and workforce issues that really do matter in your life and your career. They aren't just interesting bits of trivia or broad pictures of a social phenomenon affecting a group of people far away. The trends you will learn about here can make a huge difference in your career and in the way you go about your work. They represent the issues, challenges, and opportunities that can give you direction in planning your own career, and for better serving those you work with. They also make you a more valuable resource, because knowing and leveraging these trends can increase your ability to see what's coming, understand what you need to do to prepare, and take a lead role in shaping the training and development field. Quite simply: Knowing and using them gives you an edge.

By increasing your awareness and comprehension of workplace and workforce trends, you can better chart your own career direction, determine the skills that will be needed in your profession, and make yourself more marketable and more savvy about our field. And, you can get more excited about the possibilities ahead and claim the areas in which you want to be outstanding before others do, and even before there are job descriptions that spell out these new skill requirements in detail. Watching, understanding, and leveraging trends are excellent ways to shape your own career path.

Read through each trend with a sense of curiosity—ask yourself how you might apply new thinking and new possibilities in your current work setting—and think about how you might leverage these new ideas to grow your own expertise in days to come.

Trend 1: Learning Takes Center Stage

Can you recall the last time you went a full 24 hours without learning *something*? Chances are good that within the last day you've experienced *some* sort of learning moment. Maybe it was something new you learned—or maybe an experience confirmed for you that something you already knew still made sense. Or maybe it was a more serious situation in which you quickly had to unlearn something you used to rely on, and relearn a new approach to get an important task done or solve a thorny problem.

It doesn't really matter how or when or where it happens; continual learning is simply part of who we are and what we do.

In the workplace, the focus on learning has taken on even more urgency and importance, and it's become more critical than we've ever known it to be before. As workers, and as professionals in the training and development field, the importance of learning may seem like simply a given; it's easy to take learning for granted as something operating in the background as we go about our workday.

But acknowledging the importance of learning isn't enough—not if we're serious about making a difference in our own career and in the success of the organization and the people we serve. Rather than thinking of "learning" as simply a part of what we do, think of it as LEARNING[10]. Learning is bigger, more vital, and more exciting today. And the entire way we think about learning, design learning, and provide learning opportunities to others has grown exponentially.

Within Trend #1: *Learning Takes Center Stage*, there are numerous "mini-trends," which are included here to illustrate the many ways that learning brings value to what we do each day.

Learning and Learning Technology Mini-Trends

The Exponential Growth of Learning and Its Enabling Technologies

Technology became a game changer back in the 1990s with the emergence of e-learning. From that point forward, the industry has seen the introduction of scores of technology-enabled learning tools, prompting training and development professionals to jump on the tech bandwagon and experiment with various tech-enablers and devices that may not have existed even five years earlier.

> "To stay ahead, learning professionals must embrace the new technologies that have become commonplace in everyday life and among the new generations."
>
> —Paula Ketter
> *T+D* magazine (2012)

SumTotal's (www.sumtotalsystems.com) most recent (mid-2012) update of top learning trends includes

- an integrated learning management and talent management solution, which can lead to an increase in business results

- social learning and creating an engaging social learning portal

- mobile engagement—with a focus on making mobile learning more worthwhile and effective for users

- global language—SumTotal notes that "some global businesses are moving toward the adoption of a global language that all employees will speak, read, and write to limit disparity in learning, comprehension, and business practices and to remove some of the burdens of culture awareness" (2012)

- cloud technology—the ability to use virtual servers (rather than those linked to one's own computer) to create and deliver learning initiatives.

GOOD TO KNOW! For more information on how to leverage cloud technology, check out Human Capital Media, and search for "Six Ways Cloud Technology Will Impact Learning."

Caroline Avey, author of *What Can You Expect in 2013?*, offers her ideas on learning-related trends to watch for (in the January 2013 issue of *Chief Learning Officer*):

- increased use of apps
- QR codes to enable geo-specific learning
- increased use of video, over pictures
- blending blended learning (a micro-learning model that uses hands-on and online in smaller chunks over time, rather than training "events")
- gamification to help learners practice skills and to increase engagement.

Some additional learning-related trends and tech-enablers from e-learning coach Connie Malamed's blog include

- backchannel learning
- HTML5 for mobile
- flipped learning (2013).

GOOD TO KNOW! Ms. Malamed suggests that flipped learning can be used in the workplace in several ways. For more of her ideas, use this link: http://theelearningcoach.com/.

Elliott Masie, founder of the Masie Center, a New York-based think tank that focuses on supporting organizational learning and knowledge, offers these contributions:

- a need to determine and design for variations in learning intensity
- the need to help learners build the capacity to choose the most appropriate learning options from all those available in their workplace (2012).

In a December 2012 *T+D* article, Chris Pirie, 2012 Chair of the ASTD Board of Directors, noted the huge changes we're going through right now—brought on by the proliferation of technologies and devices available—as well as all the ways they will transform learning activities. He offers this inspiration:

> Some might find that level of change scary. In reality, this is a huge opportunity for the professional training industry. These devices need rich content and scenarios to "light them up," and smart, intelligent designers to build the next generation of training apps that will help the field engineer, salesperson, medic, or student of tomorrow.

The Possibilities of Mobile Learning (M-Learning)

This learning tech trend is so big it deserves its own section, especially if we take Pat Galagan's comment to heart when she notes: "Almost anything enabled by the Internet, including learning, can be done from the palm of your hand" (2012).

Workers today are often on the move, shuttling between their office cubes, client visits, and collaboration with fellow team members. Frequently, they are on the road, in the air, or getting ready to walk into a presentation to meet with a prospective client to solve a current customer's problem. All the great information they have back on their desktop isn't available to them at that moment. But what would be useful is the ability to get up to speed in the moment or learn some helpful new information about the person they're calling on. That is why mobile learning holds such promise and is being increasingly accepted and implemented.

Elliott Masie suggests that right now, constraints on mobile learning may be more about readiness than availability. He notes that it will be critical to first make current and new content device-ready (2013). He also notes that to be effective, the content will have to be formatted properly so it can be viewed, read, and scaled across devices.

GOOD TO KNOW! According to Pat Galagan, editor-at-large for ASTD, "By 2015, human resource executives plan to leverage mobile devices not only for learning and performance support but also for coaching and mentoring employees (37 percent), micro-blogging (27 percent), augmented reality (14 percent), and mobile gaming (12 percent)." –From *Pie in the Sky to the Palm of Your Hand: The Proliferation of Devices Spurs More Mobile Learning.* (*T+D* magazine, 2012)

The Learning and Innovation Link

Innovation is one of those buzzwords getting tossed around quite a bit right now as companies strive to be competitive and successful. Yet, what does innovation entail? Michael Bills, executive director of the Innovation Initiative at the Fisher College of Business at Ohio State University, has devoted his career to studying innovation and he consults on the topic with businesses worldwide.

In an interview with Amy Franko, published online for ASTD's Workforce Development Community of Practice, Bills defines it this way: "Innovation is about top-line growth through the creation of new products and services" (2012). Bills stresses how important it is for those of us in the training and development area to help an organization understand where the world is going and how the world continues to change. He emphasizes that we need to help leadership—and the employees within an organization—by encouraging a climate that supports collaborative skills and applauds new ideas and ways of going about one's work (Franko, 2012).

GOOD TO KNOW! Kathy Gurchiek, associate editor for HR News who authored an SHRM article on motivation for innovation, offers great ideas for fostering innovation. If you are a SHRM member, you can access the content through their website.

With all these reports, research, and comments from experts stressing the value of innovation that can be enhanced through learning, it is clear that professionals in the T&D field can contribute a great deal to encouraging an innovative mindset inside an organization. Pat Galagan and Sam Herring agree as they remind us all of the value we can add, as training and development professionals, by designing learning experiences and environments that encourage innovation (2011).

What We Know About Learning Is Evolving

These days, more attention is focused on improving the ways people learn and how we can optimize learning by making use of research on how the brain functions.

Paula Ketter, editor of ASTD periodicals, challenges us to expand our roles and our skills to apply this new information:

> It is your job, as a workplace learning and performance professional, to understand how the brain works, recognize the role that the brain plays in employee performance, and value the corporate setting that helps employees function effectively and efficiently. Maximizing learning by making training compatible to how a brain learns is crucial to maximizing efficiency in the workplace (December 2012).

Just what is brain-based learning? According to Bob Lucas, writing for the ASTD Learning and Development Newsletter:

> Brain-based or brain-compatible (active) learning theory focuses on creating an opportunity in which attainment, retention, recall, and use of information is maximized. This concept incorporates the latest research on the brain and encourages application of findings to training and educational learning environments.

WATCH! For a fascinating look at how we can "cross-train" our brains for greater creativity and innovation, view Ann Herrmann-Nehdi's YouTube video.

The Brain's Influence on Learning and Effectiveness

David Rock, co-founder of the NeuroLeadership Institute, reminds us that conditions need to be right for learners to be able to access important new insights that lead to organizational successes. In an article on accessing a learner's "aha" moments (2011), Rock suggests conditions to encourage the blossoming of new ideas, including relaxation and quiet. He also suggests organizations create places and times during the workday when employees can access a sense of quiet, and have the chance to let their minds wander and free associate.

Others studying this field remind us our brains perform best when we're free from stress and pressure—because stress and pressure can lead to withdrawal and disengagement, and certainly don't bring out our best ideas.

Evaluating the Impact of Learning

Though designing, managing, and implementing successful learning initiatives are important goals, they are not enough. By themselves, they cannot contribute to the overall effectiveness of an organization or an employee. We know that. All our efforts, as training and development professionals, need to contribute to the overall effectiveness of an organization. To ensure that happens, we need to "up" our game when it comes to understanding and leveraging the right metrics to make a difference. Evaluating and measuring across the initiatives we create and implement can help us track our successes and make changes along the way. Ongoing evaluation and the use of cutting-edge metrics also makes us an equal partner with other key functions inside our organization, as it lets us guide performance improvement efforts and demonstrate our value and relevance.

GOOD TO KNOW! Ron Cowan wrote a helpful article on "10 Ways to Measure Learning Impact." If you are an ASTD member, you can access the content through astd.org.

Truly Future Learning Possibilities

Want a peek at the outer fringes of what learning might look like in the future? In Pat Galagan's future-focused *T+D* article (2012) she asks the provocative question: "How would you train a transhuman?" Clearly the learners we work with daily aren't likely to morph into some other species anytime soon. But Galagan's query offers great food for thought.

She suggests that pioneering efforts in genetics, nanotechnology, neuroscience, and pharmacology are all on the same quest: to produce a better brain. What might that mean for us in the T&D profession? Consider her speculations on just what we might see in the not-too-distant future workplace:

- learners with genetically and chemically enhanced brains pursuing their own learning agendas via technology

- transhuman teachers who can anticipate and meet any learning need

- a burgeoning of jobs for people who can develop technology to accelerate, enhance, and guide learning experiences

- training suppliers emerging from the pharmaceutical, genetic engineering, and nanotechnology industries.

Further Ideas About Technology and Learners

Obviously, when it comes to learning, one size doesn't fit all. But take that idea a bit further. The complexity of our times, coupled with the explosion of technology, has led to an increase in the number of workers who are quite likely learning in new ways that we have to consider. Authors Joe Campbell and William Finegan (2013), writing in *Training* magazine about technology-savvy workers who have never known an Internet-less world, refer to these workers as "social cyborgs."

The authors emphasize the need for us, as T&D professionals, to engage these workers. For example, we need to consider how best to leverage newer learning strategies and bring a new mindset to our work with these tech-savvy employees.

Is learning evolving? You bet. And so must we as we consider how we need to evolve to succeed in our roles of training and development professionals.

What You Need To Know

- Learning is taking center stage in the workplace, and the techniques, technologies, and tools that are changing the learning process are growing exponentially.

So What?

- Training and development professionals are poised to take the lead in helping organizations understand and leverage new ways of learning for both employer and employee success.

Why You Should Care

- It is up to us to stay on our own cutting edge and familiarize ourselves with the wide range of options for learning, along with the ability to help others choose the best and most appropriate way to learn in any given situation. This is critical if we want our work to be relevant to the individuals and organizations we serve.

Trend 2: A Culture of Connectivity

Connectivity can involve two co-workers having a meaningful interaction, or it can be part of a philosophy that helps guide an organization. It can also be a powerful tool that can help us in the training and development field to better reach and engage our learners. Bottom line? Connectivity's growing role in the workplace and in learning changes everything.

> "The force driving the most radical change in organizations today is knowledge gained and shared through social media, the great amplifier of our time."
> —Pat Galagan
> *T+D* magazine (December 2012)

How and Why Connectivity Has Become So Important

A quick scan of all the other trends in this chapter would give you this snapshot: We inhabit a highly complex, worldwide workplace that requires high-tech and high-touch skills to meet increasing demands for constant innovation and improved performance. Our co-workers and customers come from increasingly diverse backgrounds and we all depend on one another to get our work done. The one common element that ties each of these workplace realities together is the ability to connect in meaningful ways with others.

The ubiquity of social media and the digital age are certainly among the primary contributors that have pushed us toward a culture of increased connectivity. Access to widespread dissemination of information has made changes possible that we could not have imagined even 25 years ago; access has also raised expectations of more transparency and responsiveness between friends, family members, employees, organizations, and leaders everywhere. For instance, consider these scenarios:

- Customers can directly and quickly access the company that made the espresso machine they bought last night to solve the coffee-making problem they are experiencing this morning.

- Worried parents can connect with a nurse at 1:00 a.m. to check on their child's symptoms.

- Neighbors, anxious about changes in their community, can reach out to their elected officials by email or text.

We connect because we can, because we want to, and often because we are expected to do so. For those of us in training and development, the challenge is to make certain that we leverage connectivity—either technology-enabled or face to face—to increase our learners' opportunities to collaborate with one another, improve performance, and accelerate innovation.

The Benefits and Potential of Connectivity—Tech-Enhanced and Face-to-Face

Savvy companies, smart job seekers, and employees alike have embraced our newfound fascination with connectivity. There are so many ways to connect that our challenge may be to select the best channels, the right time, and the most appropriate methods for connecting with our learners—and with those to whom we report—to highlight learning, enhance its delivery, and find ways for increasing the value of connecting.

Here are some ways connectivity is reshaping people processes in the workplace. Trend #6 will go into more detail on these processes. The brief snapshot here highlights how connectivity is enhancing each of the following activities.

Recruitment

The ability to find new employees using social networks has made valuable connections possible for both the employer and the job seeker, and the tech-enhanced possibilities for connecting seem to keep getting better all the time. For example, California-based Jobvite (http://recruiting.jobvite.com/) uses social recruiting software that makes talent acquisition and employee referrals efficient and much faster than in the pre-tech recruiting days. Glassdoor.com offers candid reviews of companies from former employees and those familiar with the organization (www.glassdoor.com/Reviews/index.htm).

Engagement and Performance Feedback

We know that feedback, properly given and delivered soon after observing the behavior, is more useful than feedback given a month or two later. Yet, many systems are built around feedback that is given at performance review time—which may occur at quarterly, six-month, or yearly intervals—when the behavior in question is too old to even recall accurately. Feedback given at that time does little to boost current performance levels.

But technology changes that. Pat Galagan's (2009) article "Dude, How'd I Do?" points out that tools like Twitter and Facebook can offer far more immediate performance appraisal, especially for Gen Y and younger employees.

> Instead of waiting months for a formal review from their bosses, they're asking people in their online networks to help them learn how to improve right away…these social networkers have figured out how to shorten the learn-and-do loop and are surging ahead using tools that are part of their daily lives (Galagan, 2009).

Staying Connected to Former Employees

Savvy organizations are leveraging the power of connection with their ex-employees. Companies like Microsoft and KPMG LLP are committed to staying connected to former employees. Many do this through online alumni networks. And some organizations signal their focus on continuing to keep former employees "in the family" through adding positions like Alumni Relations Director to their HR function.

Connectivity and Partnerships

Smart organizations recognize and embrace a wide range of opportunities to connect with their employees and other stakeholders. For example, many companies are partnering with schools in various ways to forge relationships between themselves, academic institutions, and students.

Ernst & Young is one of those companies that understands the value in making connections with potential employees early. Laurie Brady is E&Y's Americas campus recruiting leader. She's active in their Emerging Leaders Summit, which brings together student leaders from across the U.S. to hear global leaders speak, and to participate in team-building and leadership-building activities. Brady lays out the challenge this way: "If other organizations want to win the war for top talent, they need to get in the game early in the student's academic lifestyle" (Pace, 2012).

GOOD TO KNOW! See the E&Y webpage for more information on their program. Check out the Emerging Leaders Summit information.

Other companies are acting as advisors and consultants to schools and universities. They are suggesting curriculum and content enhancements so that classes can offer students the skills organizations are hungry for right now.

The Challenges of Connectivity

With all of tech-enhanced connectivity's potential, some individuals continue to retain a healthy skepticism of the power of connecting through technology. They question the quality of our technology-enhanced exchanges. Sherry Turkle, author of *Alone Together* (2011), raises an important question when she asks us to consider whether the availability and use of all the new technologies is really leading us toward the kind of lives we want for ourselves.

> "The work-at-all-hours culture has eroded work-life boundaries."
>
> —Laura Vanderkam
> author of *168 Hours:*
> *You Have More Time Than You Think*

WATCH! For a fascinating look at how technology and connectivity are changing our lives, search for the TED talk by author Sherry Turkle.

Our own everyday experiences may make us wonder, as well. Talking to someone on the phone while we hear that person's new email announcements coming through may give us the impression that our phone call doesn't hold much value for the person on the other end of the line. They are using our conversation as an opportunity to multitask. Likewise, having our face-to-face discussion interrupted frequently while the person we're talking with stops to answer a cell phone call surely dampens our enthusiasm for the conversation. Both these examples can leave the impression that the person who finds technology more important than human interaction has less than stellar communication and connecting skills—all red flags in one's career portfolio.

Dan Goleman, author of the bestselling *Emotional Intelligence*, suggests another challenge of connectivity. He points out that our great tech-enabled communication tools may result in fewer face-to-face interactions. The potential problem here, especially for business leaders, in Goleman's view, is that face-to-face interactions are critical to strong emotional intelligence: a prime factor in helping organizations succeed (Kalman, 2013).

The Rise of the Hyper-Connected Worker

A study done by IDC reported in 2008 that 16 percent of workers across the world were "hyper-connected," meaning they used a minimum of seven devices for work with access to at least nine applications, while another 36 percent were deemed to be "increasingly connected," using a minimum of four devices, with personal access to six or more applications (Aducci et al., 2008).

Here's the interesting part. This research, conducted by IDC and commissioned by Nortel, posited that the 16 percent of hyper-connected individuals *plus* the addition of 36 percent of increasingly connected people together were expected to spur a 40 percent growth of the hyper-connected in the current year, 2013 (Aducci et al., 2008). Bottom line: Ignore the importance that people place on tech-enabled connectivity at your peril!

Nomo What?

Though you might not be familiar with the term, chances are good you've seen others with a condition called *nomophobia*. Here's a hint: think about all those people who can't seem to function without their cell phone close by. They are the workers, students, neighbors, or friends who seem to operate best when they're actually holding their mobile device—whether or not they're using it. Cases of nomophobia (an abbreviation for "no mobile phone phobia") are growing, and the problem is often marked by extreme anxiety if one doesn't actually have hold of their mobile device.

What does this have to do with learning and development? Cell phone obsession is like any other obsession; it can be distracting and can keep learners from focusing. Even more challenging—if one's connection to their mobile device becomes more important than that person's ability to engage in real face-to-face conversation, imagine what that might do to the quality of conversations, relationships, and decision making, especially in today's workplace that counts so much on quality interactions to get work done.

Whether it's online, offline, face-to-face, or through emerging technologies allowing us to interact with others from remote parts of the world, no one will be excused for having poor connecting and collaborating skills.

What You Need to Know

- Connectivity—the ability to connect with others—is getting easier, enabling an incredible range of options for developing quality training and learning initiatives.

- An in-depth as well as broad understanding of the possibilities of using connectivity in learning will be critical.

- As we move toward even greater demands for collaborating, the ability to connect in meaningful ways with others will surely grow exponentially.

So What?

- While connectivity offers incredible opportunities for learning and for increased collaboration with individuals, teams, and entire organizations, connectivity also requires an ability to determine how best to leverage it for improving performance and for enhancing relationship building and innovation across the organization.

Why You Should Care

- The most in-demand training and development professionals will be those who are effective in guiding the organizations they work with to create opportunities for employees at all levels to connect to learning across the organization—including reaching those who work across the globe.

Trend 3: Shifting Demographics and Increasing Diversity

Unless you've been living your life off the grid and in some remote location for the past decade or so, there is no way you could have missed at least some of the hundreds of articles, books, and talk shows devoted to describing different generations in the workplace and the implications of all these people interacting with one another. Nor could you have missed some of the scores of articles, blog posts, and feature stories on the impact of diversity for our society and our workplaces, which has led to richer life experiences and a more inclusive workplace for all of us.

> "As workers delay retirement or enter encore careers later in their life spans, a workplace can include people from a variety of generations, backgrounds, and experiences who possess different styles of thinking, learning, and working. Such diversity can present challenges but also rich opportunities for leadership and management."
>
> —*The Future of Work Report*
> Apollo Research Institute (2012)

With all this information available on increasing diversity and a widening of the generations currently in the workplace, how much reflection have you done on what shifting demographics and increased diversity means for you, as a training and development professional, and for those you serve? That is what this trend highlights.

The Demographic Mix

A decade or two ago, our focus was on the implications of having three decades working side by side: those labeled Traditionalists (born between 1925 and 1945), the Boomers (born between 1946 and 1964) and Generation X (born between 1965 and 1980). Then, more recently we realized that it would be four generations likely to work side by side—with the addition of Millennials, also referred to as Gen Y (born between 1981 and 1999).

But the changes don't stop there. In *The New Workforce* (2004), author Harriet Hankin tells us that by 2020 it's likely we will mix it up even more with the addition of Generation Z (as the media has named them): those born somewhere between 1995 and 2000 and after. Imagine: Individuals with a possible age range of more than 55 or 60 years between them working side by side!

Information on all these different generations (with the exception of Gen Z) has been covered well in other publications (see *References and Suggested Readings* for some of these titles). The focus in this trend is on considering many of the ways these four—and possibly five—generations will behave and interact to make the workplace more complex. The focus here is also on emphasizing how important it will be for T&D professionals to bring both a broad and an inclusive perspective to strategizing, developing, and implementing learning initiatives for employee and organizational success.

Diversity—Expanded in Scope to Achieve a More Inclusive Workforce

The range of diversity in the workplace today is likely much broader than most of us generally consider when we hear the word. Beyond age, race, ethnicity, religion, and sexual orientation, there are countless other dimensions to diversity including differences in learning style, types of intelligence, and ability levels, to name just a few. All these differences—and more—have to be considered if the workplace is truly to be inclusive with opportunities for all workers to learn and grow.

> "For the very first time in history, the number of workers over age 55 will surpass the number of workers ages 25 to 34. Of course, that decision is having far-reaching negative consequences for Gen Xers who want to move up and positive consequences of some employers who will have the benefit of their expertise longer."
> —The Herman Trend Alert
> (July 11, 2012)

Updates on Generational and Diversity Opportunities and Challenges

It is likely that you already have a good grasp of much of the unique contributions and concerns of the different generations in the workplace. And you probably are also aware of how diversity trends and initiatives are evolving.

The data points that follow are based on the latest research and surveys. They are meant to add to your current knowledge base on these groups and help you further refine your approaches to meeting these workers' learning needs.

Interactions Among Generations

- More than 34 percent of U.S. workers report to a younger boss (Lorenz, 2012).

- Differences in method of communicating show up across the generations as well: All groups seem to prefer face-to-face, but younger workers favor email and texting (Lorenz, 2012), while Traditionalists tend to be more formal and less spontaneous.

Generation Z

We're still speculating on what Gen Z will bring to the workplace and how they will influence training and development. Here are some hints on what we might expect:

- These preteens, teens, and young adults were born into a world shaped by 9/11, the War on Terror, and Columbine. Writer Lance Looper suggests that these individuals may focus more on social justice issues as they age, given the harsh economic recession-related issues they've grown up with.

- Because they're used to a constant flow of information accessible with a few clicks, they may be attracted to the quick answer, which might not be the best one.

Gen Y/Millennials

- A large number of Millennial workers are drawn to smaller employers, perhaps because they are interested in flexible work environments and don't believe that large corporations can offer them this option.

- According to David Ulrich (McGraw, 2012), Gen Y sees continuous sharing and collaborating via social media as a "way of life." So, it's likely they'll expect to be offered training and growth opportunities that use tech-enabled learning, available when they want it (since geographic restrictions don't apply).

- Many Millennials are experiencing what *Futurist* author Edward Cornish describes as "futurephobia" because they are growing up in the midst of so many upheavals and social and economic transformations (2010), which can make it difficult for them to think creatively about their future—including their careers.

Generation X

- They consider themselves self-reliant and searching for work-life balance.

- They may be viewed by others as skeptical and informal, and don't necessarily see value in following norms of formality, rules, and protocol (Solutions Design, 2009).

Boomers

- Companies are increasingly seeing Boomers in their workplace as an asset. For example, CVS Caremark has found that many of its customers prefer consulting with older, more experienced pharmacists about health issues. CVS Caremark has identified this as a plus and has created flexible work arrangements for their older workers (Leahy, 2012).

- The "age of concern" for applicants has risen: "Age of concern"—the point at which search consultants believe age becomes a negative factor in getting hired—has moved up to 57, according to ExecuNet's 20th annual *Executive Job Market Intelligence Report* (McCool, 2012).

The Silent Generation/Traditionalists

- A *Wall Street Journal* article noted that, for the first time since the government began tracking such numbers, "one in nine American men over the age of 75 was working in April," (Norris, 2012) and one in 20 women in that age range was in the workplace.

- They value following rules and expect that those they work with will do the same.

Here are some additional data points that go beyond generational differences and reflect recent research related to other important characteristics of our workforce that we need to take into account.

Veterans

- As of September 2012, the overall unemployment rates for returning vets was 9.7 percent, while the unemployment rate for female vets climbed to 19.9 percent (Briggs, 2012).

- Some of the perceived challenges of hiring workers with military experience include: difficulty transitioning from the structure and hierarchy in military culture to civilian workplace culture; the amount of time it takes them to adapt to a civilian workplace culture; and the tendency for them to be under qualified for positions they apply for, according to a poll taken by the Society for Human Resource Management (2010).

- Approximately 20 percent of veterans return from recent wars, including Iran and Afghanistan, with post-traumatic stress disorder (PTSD). These workers may need additional support in their workplace learning efforts.

GOOD TO KNOW! For more information on veterans and civilian employment, review the United States Department of Labor website. Search for "New Employment Initiatives for Veterans."

Gender

- More young women, discouraged about finding a job, have gone back to school. Their choice to do so may mean that they become the primary breadwinners in their families. It may also mean that they will be able to apply for and land jobs that were, in the past, more male-dominated (Schramm, 2012).

- The number of stay-at-home dads is on the rise, and their status is no longer seen as an anomaly, but more the "new normal." According to a *New York Times* article, the number of men who have chosen to stay home with their kids stands at 176,000 (Williams, A., 2012).

WATCH! For a look at the "new normal" and dads as primary caregivers, check out a video on Today.com. It is connected with the article "Stay-at-Home Dads Embrace New Family Norm."

Workers With Hidden Disabilities

- According to Grace Austin, writing in *Profiles in Diversity Journal*: "Today, one in 88 individuals is diagnosed with an autism spectrum disorder and it is estimated that one in 250 people have Asperger's Syndrome. So, whether you know it or not, if your company has 1,000 or more employees, it's likely that you already work with people with Asperger's" (2012).

- There are an estimated 10 million adults in the U.S. with ADHD (Beck, 2010); and those in the workplace diagnosed as having ADHD may be challenged to find a job, hang on to that job, and be paid the same rate as those who do not have ADHD. Individuals with ADHD may have a more difficult time focusing, and they may experience other learning-related challenges, which may affect their ability to learn.

LGBT

- The recent Catalyst article, "Lesbian, Gay, Bisexual, and Transgender Issues in the Workplace" (2012) found that close to 40 percent of "out" lesbian, gay, and bisexual respondents said that they had experienced harassment or discrimination in the workplace based on sexual orientation.

- Perceived discrimination and lack of social support has been shown to lead to career indecision in LGBT college students and may also limit their career aspirations, once they are employed.

Workers Without Digital Literacy Skills

- A 2012 report from NOVA Workforce Development noted that "in the next 10 years, almost 80 percent of U.S. jobs will require workers to know how to use a computer, search the Internet, and communicate using social networks. But today, over 20 percent of Americans lack these basic digital literacy skills."

Immigrant Workers

- The Migration Information Source (http://www.migrationinformation.org/) notes: "There were 23 million immigrants in the U.S. civilian labor force in 2010… Within the immigrant labor force, nearly half speak English less than 'very well' (as defined by the U.S. Census Bureau) and are classified as 'Limited English Proficient,' a language barrier that affects their employability and wage-earning potential" (Pandya, 2012).

The Working Poor

- A report done by the U.S. Department of Labor noted that in 2010, the Census Bureau found that "10.5 million individuals were among the 'working poor,' meaning they were living below the official poverty line, and the ratio of the working poor to all individuals in the labor force was 7.2 percent."

Expatriate Workers Returning Home

- According to Transition Dynamics, one of the concerns of workers returning to their "home" workplace after the completion of an expat assignment is that they won't be able to demonstrate the knowledge and skills they gained during that assignment (Ramsey and Schaetti, 1999).

What You Need to Know

- Organizations will employ an increasingly diverse workforce. Age-wise, our workplaces will see as many as five generations working next to one another. Additionally, diversity will continue to bring together workers with a wider range of backgrounds, cultures, and ways of working than ever before.

So What?

- A more diverse workforce can offer many advantages to an organization.

- At the same time, to make certain that all employees are able to contribute their talents and strengths, it will be important to take into consideration the different backgrounds and styles of learning and interacting when developing T&D initiatives.

Why You Should Care

- Training and development professionals can offer key skills to help organizations understand, value, and leverage the unique talents of a diverse workforce.

- Organizations will continue to need guidance and support in making the most of each employee's contributions. Professionals in our field can develop initiatives, coach managers, and model behaviors that are important to forward-thinking, innovative, and inclusive workplaces.

Trend 4: Globalization 3.0

"Globalization" is a word that seems to show up everywhere, and seems to get blamed—or praised—for any event happening anywhere on the planet. It is also a term that we see and hear frequently in articles and speeches about the significant changes going on in our workplace. Yet, though we use the word frequently, what do we know about how it affects our work in training and development?

"In the global, technologically connected economy, employers can find skilled workers almost anywhere. To compete and stay employable, workers must be lifelong learners who continue to develop higher-order thinking skills and demonstrate that they can adopt new technology."

—ASTD Staff
"Five Workplace Trends" (2012)

The Evolution of Globalization

Globalization isn't new. If you read Thomas Friedman's book, *The World Is Flat*, then you know Friedman's take on globalization's evolution. For those who may not have read his book, Friedman believes that in the past 500+ years, we've evolved from Globalization 1.0 to Globalization 3.0 (2005).

Globalization 3.0, a period that began less than 15 years ago, according to Friedman, represents the world we live in now. This is a world in which individuals and groups, aided by technology, are empowered to accomplish things never before possible.

Interested in brushing up on your Italian? Hire your own tutor from Tuscany and practice with him via Skype. Wonder what your job options might be in Singapore? Connect with your colleagues living and working there via social media and ask them. Wish you could go to that conference in Warsaw next month? "Virtual" attendance is a definite possibility through multiple tech-related tools.

Bottom line: Globalization 3.0 expands the possibilities for individuals around the world, and it changes T&D in huge ways.

What does globalization mean for us and for the employees, coaching clients, and organizations we serve? Perhaps more than anything else, it means we have to "up" our knowledge and skill base and look beyond our own borders at the larger world to be better informed and savvy about the learning needs, challenges, and opportunities across the globe.

The Shift to a Worldwide Workplace Talent Pool

We've been telling the clients we coach in their job search, as well as the employees we coach for a promotion, that their competition for the new spot they want is no longer just their neighbor down the street—it's now also a fellow professional on the other side of the world. We're accustomed to preparing our clients for these new workplace realities, including a global pool of talent. But we need to go further.

A larger pool of talent continues to ratchet up the challenges. Oxford Economics partnered with Towers Watson and others (2012) to create an in-depth report, *Global Talent 2021*, which highlights the fact that "the talent pool is moving from industrial to emerging markets, with the fastest growing annual talent pools predicted to be in India, Brazil, Indonesia, Turkey, and China." Consider what that means for competition for jobs and what it means for preparing our students and workers to compete for global assignments.

Global Skills Needed for a Global Workplace

In Trend #8, you will read more about the range of skills that have been identified as critical for today's and tomorrow's workers. This trend, globalization, highlights four broad areas and their accompanying skill sets, where, according to the Oxford Economics and Towers Watson report (2012), skills will be in the highest demand in the *global* workplace. These include

1. Digital skills:

   - digital business skills

   - ability to work virtually

   - understanding of corporate IT software and software systems

   - digital design skills

   - ability to use social media and Web 2.0.

2. Agile thinking skills:

   - ability to consider and prepare for multiple scenarios

   - innovation

   - dealing with complexity and ambiguity

   - managing paradoxes, balancing opposing views

   - ability to see the big picture.

3. Interpersonal and communication skills:

   - co-creativity and brainstorming

   - relationship building (with customers)

   - teaming (including virtual teaming)

   - collaboration

   - oral and written communication.

4. Global operating skills:

   - ability to manage diverse employees

   - understanding international markets

   - ability to work in multiple overseas locations

   - foreign language skills

   - cultural sensitivity.

The report also notes that these skills will be needed, not just by executives, but by employees at all levels who wish to be successful in a global marketplace and workplace.

The Society for Human Resource Management (SHRM) has also researched what global characteristics are needed for leaders and multicultural teams to be successful. They suggest a training process that emphasizes a global perspective is critical. This perspective calls for "integrating all culturally diverse and geographically dispersed employees into one unified team or unit" (Gurchiek, 2011).

Ernst & Young's Laurie Brady, one of the leaders of E&Y's youth development leadership programs, has also stressed the global mindset requirement for career success: She believes it is critical for organizations to support this in the students they interact with in their E&Y programs (Pace, 2012).

Globalization and the Changing Expat Experience

Dana Mattioli, writing in *The Wall Street Journal* (2009), describes an interesting dilemma for expats from other countries who have come to the U.S. for work and advancement. Tough economic times in this country, including salary and promotion freezes, along with visa issues, and new job possibilities outside the U.S., are making these workers who have homes elsewhere rethink their decision to stay in the United States and consider a move back to their home country instead.

Closer to home, U.S. expats also face increased challenges. In the past, an overseas assignment may have been more of a "helicoptering in and out of locations" experience, as Laura Levenson, director of consulting services for Weichert Relocation Resources, puts it (Krell, 2012). But that is not the case today, if the employee wants to be successful.

A study featured in *HR Magazine* notes the complexity of succeeding in another culture that goes beyond just going there and simply doing one's job. Research shows that those employees who can both adapt to the local environment of their assignment and stay connected with their home environment at the same time have a much more successful experience and show higher performance during their time away (Krell, 2012).

How do we help employees gain this "integrative complexity" that the researchers describe as they prepare for an overseas assignment? Simply making cross-cultural training available for those taking on an international assignment probably isn't enough. Nor is a quick "crash course" in the customs and language of a different culture sufficient. Successful companies make cross-cultural training mandatory and take steps to make certain this training is effective. This also includes more in-depth training and support than simply offering readings and a bit of time spent with a trainer. In these days of increased mobility, professionals in training and development need to identify ways to help expat employees succeed before, during, and after their assignments when they come back home again.

Global Nomads on the Rise

We're seeing a rise in global mobility among some savvy workers. According to Tom Starner, writing for *Human Resource Executive Online*, a survey done by Mercer (2012) indicated that new business ventures, developing global leadership talent, and other factors have enticed more workers into becoming "global nomads."

Just like workers everywhere, they need to stay at the top of their game if they want to continue to be considered for such assignments. T&D professionals need to design learning interventions that fit their learning style, location, and learning challenges.

Challenges of Training/Learning in a Global Setting

Enthusiasm and effort are high as corporations expand their global workforce and as they get virtual teams from across the globe to work together. But even with this enthusiasm and desire to collaborate, there are challenges to getting these groups to perform well together. According to a SHRM survey, these challenges include:

- time differences
- virtual team leadership
- cultural norms
- building team relationships
- distribution of work (2012).

Each of these challenges must be addressed, and professionals in training and development can be key resources in turning these concerns into opportunities for individual and organizational success.

Providing Learning to a Global Workforce

In today's worldwide workplace, with more organizations opening business units, regional centers, and plants around the globe, it is imperative that the skills of employees across an organization are regularly updated, improved, and refined. The ongoing strategic learning and development they receive should position their organization for success in achieving its goals and moving its strategy forward, and position the workers as skilled and savvy global workers.

Providing learning to a global workforce is not easy. The ASTD research report, *The Global Workplace: Learning Beyond Borders* (2012) developed jointly by ASTD and the Institute for Corporate Productivity (i4cp), took a close look at the current state of the delivery of global learning, along with its challenges, opportunities, barriers, and enablers. Here is how they summarize the challenge:

> There is much more to global learning and development than simply developing and delivering content for regions outside an organization's headquarters. Many considerations must be taken into account to establish and sustain an effective global learning and development function, including resources, governmental issues, cultural concerns, organizational design, and delivery approaches.

The report also looked at the qualities that T&D professionals should possess to be successful in their roles of creating or sustaining a successful global learning initiative. Qualities that were mentioned include

- high level of adaptation

- patience

- cultural intelligence

- flexibility

- open-mindedness

- adeptness at relationship building and diplomacy

- understanding of the need for compromise, at times, to be able to make thoughtful, informed decisions.

Any professional who becomes involved in designing and delivering learning to a global workforce needs to be keenly aware of the challenges that go along with this effort. That is why the qualities listed above are so important.

 **GOOD TO KNOW!** If you are anticipating adding the delivery of learning globally to your areas of strength, this ASTD study offers a current, cutting-edge look at how it's being done and it gives you an important heads-up in planning out how you and those you serve can succeed. To find the report, search on store.astd.org for *The Global Workplace: Learning Beyond Borders.*

What You Need to Know:

- Globalization affects the skills that are needed to be successful in a global workplace.

- It also requires finding talent and developing talent in new ways.

- U.S. workers need help in navigating the global workplace and in collaborating with global team members.

So What?

- As a training and development professional, you may work in other parts of the globe or you may train or coach others as they prepare for international assignments.

Why You Should Care

- Your own global mindset and your updated knowledge of what's needed both in the U.S. and outside its borders will determine your own success and that of the workers and organizations you serve.

- If you want to stand out in your field, become a globally savvy professional!

Trend 5: The Impact of Economic Turmoil and Recession

If you're wondering how American workers are doing post-recession, why not ask the workers themselves?

That is what the Heldrich Center for Workforce Development did. The Rutgers University Heldrich Center, a research and policy center, has published a report, *Diminished Lives and Futures: A Portrait of America in the Great-Recession Era* (2013). It sums up the impact of the Great Recession and its resulting economic turmoil, as workers and families continue to try and recover from this turbulent period in Americans' lives. The report makes evident the challenges American workers and their families still face.

> "We're in the midst of a perfect storm: a Great Recession that has caused a sharp increase in unemployment and a Great Inflection—a merger of the information technology revolution and globalization that is simultaneously wiping out many decent-wage, middle-skilled jobs and replacing them with decent-wage, high-skilled jobs."
> —Thomas Friedman
> *The New York Times* (2012)

Here are some of the key findings from their just-released study (2013):

- The Great Recession left an indelible imprint on the American workforce. Approximately 8.7 million jobs were lost between the start of the recession in December 2007 through early 2010.

- Those who were laid off during the recession but were fortunate enough to find new employment are generally settling for less in their new position. Forty-eight percent say their current job is a step down from the one they held before the recession hit. Fifty-four percent report lower pay in their new job compared to the job they held before being laid off.

- Today, three in five believe there is a "new normal" for economic conditions in the United States, and that it is a major step down.

- Three times as many people believe the days when workers could feel secure in their jobs is a thing of the past than believe job security is possible in present day America.

- Not only does the public not see signs of economic recovery now, they don't see it in the near future either.

- For those laid off during the recession, 46 percent reported taking a job that was below their skill/education level.

GOOD TO KNOW! For the full report, search for *Diminished Lives and Futures: A Portrait of America in the Great-Recession Era.*

While we can read these disheartening statistics and doubt the American workers' ability to bounce back, we also need to know that many—even those who are still unemployed—hold some optimism of being able to make a comeback. As T&D professionals, we can help these individuals—as well as downsized organizations—to recover. But first, it's important to get a fuller picture of the workplace milieu at the present time.

Changes in the Employer-Employee Relationship

The current disruption of the employer-employee relationship is a leftover from what workers experienced as a result of the 2006–2008 recession—and it's a disruption that many individuals continue to experience today if they haven't yet been called back to work, or, if they have been called back but their hours or benefits have been cut. This fracture in the relationship creates a sense of betrayal for some as workers realize that many of their jobs are not ever coming back.

Added to this challenge is the fact that many employers are reluctant to increase their workforces, increase their training budgets, or launch new initiatives that could help workers gain new skills until they feel the time is right to do so. Taken all together, these challenges contribute to a further erosion of the employer-employee relationship.

Employees are aware of their companies' reluctance to bring on more workers and extend cutbacks on training, development, and other professional development initiatives. Their awareness means that employees may feel reluctant to go the extra mile, show commitment and engagement, or pitch in to help their organizations grow.

Tired and over-worked employees, trying to function with reduced resources, may also be the first ones out the door as the economy recovers. A report by Calling Brands sums the situation up well when it suggests that the current workplace uncertainty, coupled with job insecurity, tends to make some employees look more at their work as temporary until something better comes along (2012).

The Survivors: Worried Workers

It isn't just the unemployed who are challenged. Those employees who didn't get pink slips during a downsizing aren't feeling particularly secure. These people are variously described as the "working worried" (Williams, C., 2009), as those suffering from "recession rumination" (Kellogg, 2008), or simply as "survivors," who are doing the work of at least one or two others, in addition to their own job. Many of these working worried are likely to feel a bit anxious, distracted, tired, and wondering if they might be next. And they cannot and should not be ignored.

As T&D professionals, we see these people every day. They are in the classes we teach, the groups we facilitate, the teams we help our organizations to build, and in the coaching sessions we offer to provide them with support and career direction.

We can help worried workers find solid footing by informing them of resources, making them aware of training that can help them "up-skill," and giving them career tools to explore and prepare for what's next.

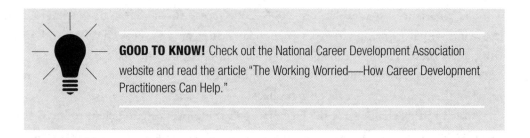

GOOD TO KNOW! Check out the National Career Development Association website and read the article "The Working Worried—How Career Development Practitioners Can Help."

Additional issues related to the fallout from the recession and the economic turmoil it generated still challenge many workers. Here are some of the challenges we may encounter in the employees we work with and the organizations we serve.

Fatigue

Claire Caruso and Roger Rosa, writing for the Centers for Disease Control and Prevention NIOSH Science Blog, commented on research done by the National Institute for Occupational Safety and Health (NIOSH). The report found that 30 percent of U.S. workers are getting less than the seven to nine hours a night recommended by the National Sleep Foundation (2012). The result? Aside from the risks to their health, these workers make mistakes, their productivity goes down, and their absenteeism and presenteeism go up. Why so much fatigue? According to Dori Meinert, writing in *HR Magazine*, it may be because of the pressure to hold down two jobs to deal with financial pressures, or it may be because of an increased need to always be available to their employer, since technology makes that possible (2012).

The Effects of "Supercommuting"

USA Today reported that the number of workers who are "supercommuters"—those who work in a different city than they live and travel long distances to get to work—is on the rise. According to the article, the reason for the spike in those who make these marathon commutes is, in large part, because of the Great Recession, with its slow economic recovery, and the current conditions in the housing market (Jones, 2012).

Stress

The ripple effects of layoffs cause stress to the survivors of an organization's downsizing initiatives; those who do not get let go from their positions often end up doing the work of two or three other downsized employees. Therefore, it's likely that the survivors could benefit from support. Yet, many companies are also cutting back on programs like work-life initiatives: programs that could really benefit those survivors who are running on empty.

GOOD TO KNOW! An interesting finding from a recent WorkTrends report by D'Mello (Kenexa 2011–2012) found that employees who reported higher levels of training and development satisfaction also reported lower levels of stress.

Job Insecurity

New employees are likely to feel insecure for quite a while into the economic recovery. This is particularly true when the worker is a new employee in an organization that has been demoralized by cuts and downsizing. Katherine Hobson, writing in *U.S. News & World Report* (2009), noted that job insecurity can be as bad for one's health as a job loss itself, or as bad as a serious illness.

The Underemployed

We already know that many of the jobs that were around pre-recession aren't coming back. Some of that is due to technology, and some to the reluctance of employers to step up their hiring just yet. Additionally, more people are graduating with a baccalaureate degree—more than the number of new jobs that require college degrees.

GOOD TO KNOW! For more information on this topic, check about.com, and search for "underemployment rate."

In a work world of reduced jobs that pay a livable wage, many people are working at jobs for which they are overqualified. That means they are underemployed: working less than full-time, or working in jobs that don't make use of their training or skills.

The challenges for these workers include trying to stay motivated in jobs they consider dead-ends—with no hope of promotion—as well as trying to job hunt while holding down two (or more) part-time positions that generally don't include benefits or insurance.

More of a Mix in Who Does the Work

Because many employers don't yet feel comfortable enough to invest in hiring many workers, more organizations are looking to alternatives in staffing, including the use of part-time and contract workers.

> "The recession brought such significant operational and financial duress for U.S. companies that the business model of the future will rely heavily upon the ability to be insulated from economic downturns."
> —Jim Link from Ranstad
> (Sept. 18, 2012)

Since more organizations are opting to use temporary and part-time workers in their workforce mix, T&D professionals need to consider how to integrate these workers into organizational training initiatives. This is especially important as the term of a temporary assignment may extend longer than it did in the past, and such assignments now cross several functional areas and are found at all levels within an organization.

Elliott Masie has weighed in on this topic and suggests that T&D professionals need to consider the implications for learning for this population within an organization (2012). If more organizations choose to use this staffing model more frequently, what are the opportunities for T&D professionals to help their organizations and the temp workers to succeed?

Other Significant Residual Effects of the Recession

One of the interesting byproducts of the recession is that it has masked a stark reality of the employment/skills challenge we now face. During the time that the recession was going on—a time when more low-skilled or semi-skilled jobs were created during the housing/financial bubble—the labor market was shifting. So were requirements for the newer jobs that were being created, especially those enabled by technology. The result is that post-recession, low-skilled and semi-skilled jobs have disappeared. Now, it's the "high-skilled" people who have the best chances of finding work (Gordon, 2012).

Another residual effect of the recession is the ongoing retirement anxiety. According to a report titled *Retirement Readiness of Generation X*, many Gen X and young Boomers are struggling with planning for retirement (Insured Retirement Institute, 2012).

The Lost Generation

An article by Jennifer Schramm captures the consequences of companies' reluctance to hire full-time employees and instead, look to other hiring models. Writing in *HR Magazine*, she notes:

> College students are taking longer to earn a degree, thus beginning their working lives years later than previous generations. This was exacerbated during the recession, when many young people either postponed work to continue their studies or spent their first few years after school unemployed. More broadly, the long recession may have led to a lost generation, where young people in their prime 'innovative years' will have difficulty reaching their full potential. This could have lasting effects in a range of industries and organizations of all sizes, affecting leadership development strategies and potential contributions of new entrants to the workplace (2011).

What You Need to Know

- Workers are still feeling the effects of the Great Recession—and may appear overly cautious and sometimes risk-averse as they go about their work.

- Employee loyalty may not show up as much as it did in the past, but workers are still truly interested in working for an organization that respects them and makes use of their talents and skills.

- Unemployed and underemployed workers may be losing their ability to contribute their strongest skills and knowledge.

So What?

- Engaging learners may, at times, be challenging. However, helping learners see the value of the initiative and how it can affect their performance and success as well as their employers' can be extremely helpful.

Why You Should Care

- Acknowledging learners' reluctance or concerns shows them that they "matter"—and goes a long way to engaging them in whatever program you are proposing.

Trend 6: The Talent Trifecta: Recruiting for Agility, Fostering Engagement, and Retaining Knowledge

Jeffrey A. Joerres, CEO of ManpowerGroup, says that we've moved beyond the Information Age to the Human Age, and individuals, with their talents and skill sets, will be the most important asset to businesses today and tomorrow (2011).

In another sign of workers gaining prominence as the key asset for companies, the website of the Association of Executive Search Consultants (www.aesc.org) recently highlighted a speech that Adrian Wooldridge of *The Economist* was to give at their annual meeting. The description of the speech included how Wooldridge would "demonstrate why companies now need people more than people need companies."

> "When you think about motivating people, you have to remember that it's an intrinsic thing—it's important for any employee to know that 'my employer supports my training and development in difficult times.' It is also critical to retention to motivate staff and provide them with that development support. Developing people means going the extra step, and I think that's why people stay with an organization."
>
> —Lorelle Swader, Director, APA/HRDR, American Library Association

The State of Talent Management

Talent, and every aspect of finding it, growing it, and keeping it, is central to the success of all organizations today. Books, online discussions, blogs, speeches, and even the front page of your local newspaper mentions talent as a key priority, a top challenge, and the hot topic of the day, the week, and the month. Bottom line? Talent matters.

Talent management—often considered shorthand for the ability to have the right people, with the right skills, in the right jobs, at the right time—is an ongoing effort for every organization that wants to remain competitive today. However, integrated talent management, seen as the most effective way to build organizational capability, appears to be more an aspiration than an actuality for many organizations. There are many reasons for this, but chief among the challenges is the fact that an integrated approach—involving many different parts of an organization—is not easy.

Talent management efforts have been around for quite a while. All of an organization's efforts to recruit the right people, give them the right training, and provide opportunities for them to add to a company's bottom line are focused on building a strong talent pool. But today, the ability to do these things and do them quickly is becoming much more complex. The old days of "silos" in which one department recruited, another hired, another focused on development, while yet one more area dealt with benefits, compensation, and ultimately the retirement of employees, cannot work in the current workplace. As Kevin Oakes and Pat Galagan (2011) have noted in *The Executive Guide to Integrated Talent Management*, discrete talent-related practices don't make sense in a fast-moving world.

Not only is an integrated talent management approach needed to speed the process up; even more important, the whole process needs to be woven into the fabric of an organization and aligned with its mission so that new and experienced workers alike can more effectively contribute to a company's success. And here is the great news: T&D professionals can play a huge role in facilitating the effective deployment of human capital.

While there are many talent-related concerns on the minds of those in Human Resources and T&D functions, the focus here is on the relationship between the talent trifecta of recruiting, engaging, and retaining workers on one hand, and learning, on the other hand. Training and development professionals need to consider these three functions, and how they can leverage their role to design and deliver successful T&D initiatives that support talent management efforts.

Why an Integrated Approach to Talent Management Is Vital

It's nearly impossible to separate out activities and priorities for supporting and developing the workforce in today's organizations. You can't look at recruitment as a separate activity that, once done, will guarantee a positive impact on an organization's performance. Nor can you focus solely on keeping employees engaged while they are part of an organization, and then simply wish them well and wave good-bye when they leave. To do so would mean starting from scratch to build up a company's reserves of knowledge and skill all over again.

The three related activities mentioned in this trend work together to ensure a robust workforce and a rich pipeline. T&D professionals can contribute to the success of each.

Recruitment

Recruiting the right talent for positions across an organization needs to take into account several factors to make certain it is done right. One of these factors, so important in today's workplace, is agility. Agility really isn't one single trait, but rather a cluster of skills and a way of looking at life and its challenges.

It's no longer enough for us—or for those who are being recruited—to demonstrate a willingness or an ability to "change" and "adapt." That's a basic requirement. Beyond that, an individual worker needs to demonstrate the ability to be agile on an ongoing basis—no matter what. To use the words of writer Lisa Haneberg (2011), employees need to have the ability to "zig and zag," and do so with ease.

Once organizations have recruited workers who fill the important criteria and demonstrate agility, then T&D professionals need to continue adding to the skills of these workers by providing initiatives and guidance, so that everyone in the organization can hone their agility skills further.

LISTEN! For more on agility, listen to the ASTD podcast at www.astd.org. Search *T+D* podcasts to find "Training for Agility."

Closely linked to agility is the challenge of living in a VUCA (volatile, uncertain, complex, and ambiguous) world. In a chaotic-ever-changing workplace, the old 20th-century model of identifying, hiring, and keeping the right employees for jobs that will remain stable over time doesn't work. According to John Sullivan, thought leader in HR and well known for his expertise in recruiting, "…the question for talent leadership becomes, 'How do you effectively hire, develop, place, and retain individuals and leaders in the volatile environment where literally everything changes in months rather than years?'" (2012).

One way to answer Dr. Sullivan's question is to recruit workers who demonstrate agility related to learning. According to Joyce Gioia, learning agility "is the ease with which an individual can acquire new information and skills" (Herman Trend Alert, 2012).

Engagement

Engagement is a key driver in today's workplace. While there are several definitions of engagement, the one from a report by Aon Hewitt captures it well: "Aon Hewitt defines engagement as the state of emotional and intellectual involvement that motivates employees to do their best work" (2012).

Aon Hewitt, like similar organizations that research engagement, notes that engaged employees have higher performance. In a recent study, they found several interesting points:

- Four employees out of 10 are not engaged worldwide.

- Employees' motivation to stay and exert extra effort falls short.

- Career opportunities, recognition, and organizational reputation are consistently top engagement drivers (2012).

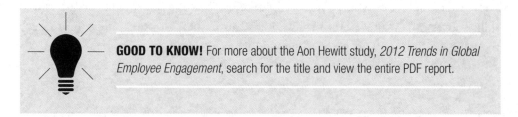

GOOD TO KNOW! For more about the Aon Hewitt study, *2012 Trends in Global Employee Engagement*, search for the title and view the entire PDF report.

Retention

Retention is a hot button word right now—for both employers and employees. Employees are weighing their options as the economy continues to improve: Should they stay where they are and seek opportunities to "grow in place"? Or should they put out word that they're open to new career opportunities elsewhere? Likewise, employers are investing time and dollars in keeping their talent from walking out the door. They're doing everything from honing their internal brand to make it more inspiring to current employees, to putting more efforts into recognition programs. Aside from helping HR keep track of retention-related metrics, what can training and development do to make a difference?

T&D professionals can play a significant role here. An article by Rieva Lesonsky offers one possible solution. She suggests that when it's not possible to give raises, it may help to offer training instead. According to a survey cited in the article, employer-provided training increases employee job satisfaction as much as getting a 17.7 percent raise (2012).

What happens if an organization cannot retain the employee but wants to retain the knowledge and know-how of that employee? Organizations use various tools to make sure important information doesn't "walk out the door." Here are some of them.

Some organizations have employees videotaped—using an interview format or other creative format—to share how they learned to approach certain tasks, master certain competencies, or apply previously learned information to a new problem.

Techniques like "soft-knowledge interviews" and mind mapping with departing employees are methods that consultant John Borchardt uses to make certain that important knowledge can be "captured" and shared with new employees who come on board—especially if the new employees are from different industries (Thilmany, 2008). Other techniques include asking soon-to-be retirees to train replacements, and also asking them to volunteer or be "on-call" for new employees who may want to seek their "deep smarts" (which can include equal parts knowledge, information, skills, and wisdom accumulated over a long tenure with a particular organization).

Lost knowledge is not just a challenge when more senior employees opt for retirement. Within the tech sector, for example, with so much changing so rapidly, knowledge can be lost when a younger worker with special knowledge or specialized skills moves on. Again, T&D professionals can be part of the strategizing to keep these high-skilled workers engaged, growing, and retained.

GOOD TO KNOW! For a look at the topic of increased voluntary turnover and its impact, view the full report on this subject from PriceWaterhouseCoopers. Search for the title to view the entire report: *Results From PwC Saratoga's 2012/2013 US Human Capital Effectiveness Report: State of the Workforce.*

There are additional challenges that are important to recognize. Beyond citing better compensation as a reason for leaving, some employees may be harder to hang on to because they want more challenges or stretch assignments. Or, they may have managers who don't quite know how to nourish their talent. Here is another place where training and development professionals can make a difference.

Additional Tools to Win the Talent Trifecta

Mentoring

Mentoring is being redefined to better meet engagement goals, and the approaches used in mentoring are broad enough to cover a wide range of methods and models—tech-enabled or not. Additionally, "redefined" mentoring approaches don't assume that only the most senior employees in an organization will mentor the chosen youngest-in-tenure new hires.

Mentoring is also a tool that can help new and early career employees accelerate their time to competency, and can be used as a strategy to help workers become and remain engaged with an employer. Feedback, when it's offered through technology-enhanced tools, can be given in a way that is more blunt, in what author Jeanne Meister calls "anonymous mentoring" (Corner, 2012).

Coaching

Alexandra Levit, author and nationally syndicated careers columnist, pointed out recently that 55 percent of American workers in 2012 were dissatisfied with their jobs. That figure alone should be proof enough that coaching could help—especially with high-potential, talented employees. Levit suggests offering retention coaching focused on educating top performers to make them more aware of available resources (2012). They can learn smart strategies to reignite their passion for their current position, or for other available work options inside their organization.

> "Mentoring helps the new employee learn the lay of the land: the informal culture of an organization. A good mentor can help open doors and provide counsel for the junior employee to avoid land mines, such as accidently saying the wrong thing. Mentoring also helps to build relationships and loyalty to the organization."
>
> —Sylvia Benatti,
> co-author of the November 2012 *T+D* article "An Intergenerational Approach to Strengthening Organizational Talent"

Career and Ongoing Professional Development

When it comes to promoting career development within an organization, Dr. B. Lynn Ware, CEO of California-based Integral Talent Systems, Inc., suggests that T&D professionals can be a key resource for their employer's recruitment and retention efforts.

Dr. Ware notes:

> Training and development professionals can change the mindset inside organizations about what development includes. They can help organizations figure out how employees can get training while they are on the

job through informal learning. They can also take the lead in determining how technology can support learning within their organizations.

Additionally, she suggests that it is in an employer's best interest to promote career development and ongoing learning because "companies who are known for having development cultures are going to be more attractive to potential employees, especially younger workers" (2013).

Helping Employees Find Purpose in Their Work

Purpose can be a key driver across all three activities: recruitment, engagement, and retention. In a Calling Brands survey, 58 percent of U.S. workers said they'd favor "joining an organization that had a clear corporate purpose, and 65 percent of workers worldwide on average said that a company with a declared 'purpose' would get them to go the extra mile in their jobs" (2012).

Harriet Hankin, author of *The New Workforce*, agrees. She notes the need for a "higher purpose" in the workplace and explains:

> A paycheck is not the only thing that employees want. Studies show they also seek a spiritual component, which includes personal growth, balance, and meaningful purpose. Organizations that champion trust, individual respect, and ethical conduct will build committed workforces and creative thinkers (2005).

Targeted Activities to Support Talent

Just like anything else, one size/style/method of engaging, developing, and retaining workers does not fit all—or even most. The multigeneration, widely diverse workforce will need to be recruited, engaged, and retained in ways that matter to them. Consider these points as you support different segments of the workforce.

For recruiting, engaging, and retaining Gen Y/Millennial workers:

- Dan Schawbel, founder and managing partner of Millennial Branding, notes that Gen Y workers are entrepreneurial and want to make a positive impact, share their ideas, and be part of meaningful discussions (2012).

- Many Gen Y workers prefer more flexible, less traditional work hours. They tend to take work home with them and therefore, aren't really interested in conforming to a traditional office schedule.

- Millennials crave feedback. Give it to them frequently. Just be certain it is constructive feedback that centers on something meaningful, so they can put it to use.

For recruiting, engaging, and retaining Gen X workers:

- The organization Achievers (www.achievers.com) recommends that organizations review their recognition program. They point out that peer-to-peer recognition, results-based recognition, and social recognition have the potential to ignite engagement for Gen X and Gen Y.

- With numerous studies suggesting that Generation X has lost trust in leadership, it is important that bosses, supervisors, and senior leaders be clear, up front, and willing to share as much information as they can.

- Because many Generation X workers feel "stuck" in their positions, offer career development initiatives that show them an increased range of options within their organization.

For recruiting, engaging, and retaining Boomer workers:

- John Rossheim recommends employers highlight the value of their decades of experience, consider them for project-based work, use different sourcing tactics to find them, and consider flexible work arrangements that will appeal to them (2012).

- A manpower study found that only 14 percent of employers worldwide had a strategy for recruiting older workers, and only 21 percent had a strategy for retaining them. Companies need to replace any negative stereotypes they have about older workers (such as their low high-tech skills, the notion that they'll cost the organization more), as these untrue assumptions will not help with either recruitment or engagement of older workers (Casey, 2010).

- Shannon Bowen-Sted, of Canadian company BOWEN Workforce Solutions, says it takes three new workers to replace one knowledgeable and skilled mature worker (Boudreau, 2011). That's a good reason for organizations to make certain they are "friendly" to older workers.

For recruiting, engaging, and retaining the Traditionalist workers:

- Because older workers have often been with a company for many years, make use of their knowledge; encourage them to share information about the company culture and identify ways they might help train new employees.

- Consider flexible schedules, which are appreciated by this cohort.

- Respect for all they have contributed is important to this group. Consider ways that you and your organization can demonstrate this respect.

For recruiting, engaging, and retaining Gen Z (who aren't yet in the workforce, but will be soon): We can't yet know exactly what Gen Z will be looking for in their workplaces. But we have hints about how best to recruit and engage them.

- Given their shorter attention span, offer informal and incidental learning opportunities.
- This group, known for being "digital natives," are quite tech savvy. Take this into account in their assignments.

What You Need to Know

- An increasingly diverse workforce requires newer strategies for all three elements of talent building, including recruiting, engaging, and retaining.

- Employees whose unique perspective and contributions are recognized will be much more likely to engage in any programs you create.

So What?

- T&D professionals are expected to be able to tailor learning initiatives to meet the needs of a wide range of learners/employees.

- Training and development can educate and guide organizations in developing programs that build the talent pipeline in all three areas.

Why You Should Care

- Your ability to nurture the strengths and leverage the talents within your diverse workforce will demonstrate your value to your organization.

Trend 7: The (r)Evolution of the American Worker

While it may appear a bit pessimistic, *Crunch Time*, a report by Calling Brands, suggests that today's workers are "less loyal, more demanding, and more suspicious about the aims and conduct of business." The report describes workers as having "a whole new set of values and priorities that rarely align with the traditional needs of the employer" (2012).

You may or may not agree with this analysis; however, it's likely you would agree that today's workers (across industries, job titles, and employment levels) have changed the way they view their work, their job security, and their expectations about what they want their work to provide. On the heels of the Great Recession, large-scale downsizing, and the uncertainty of the economy, it makes sense that most workers want to do good work for their employers on one hand, while trying their best to do what's best for themselves and their families on the other hand.

One theme that continues to come up in stories, research, and the everyday experiences of most workers is an increased desire for purpose and meaning in their work. Given how much time workers are on the job, and the increasing demands on them to do more with less, work longer hours, take shorter vacations, and "up-skill" (sometimes without their company picking up the tab), hardworking people want something more back. Workers realize that even regularly scheduled raises aren't assured as companies announce pay freezes and furloughs. But that doesn't mean they don't want, or expect, something more in return for continuing to produce in tough times.

The significant changes in our economy and workplace have combined to create a new workforce participant: one who has witnessed the workplace turmoil, learned (or is currently trying to learn) the technologies, mastered the shifting rules, accepted the new expectations, and shape-shifted to survive and thrive in this radically new environment.

Looking for More AND Less

Workers are well aware of the challenges their employers are facing. But they still have expectations that include more opportunities to learn, use their strengths, and build their skill base. The other "more" that employees are looking for is flexibility.

As for the "less" that employees are looking for—most would opt for less of a heavy workload, less of being asked to pro-

> "Whether because of newfound austerity or a broader disillusionment with consumerism, employees are seeking more intangible benefits from their jobs beyond pay, benefits, and career prospects…Employees are far more concerned with quality of life issues, in particular with getting the right work-life balance."
>
> —Calling Brands
> *Crunch Time* report (2012)

duce more with fewer resources, and less pressure to be in constant "change-ready" mode 24/7.

Recent research shows that employees who are overloaded on a long-term basis suffer physically and mentally. Their production, engagement, and the quality of work will go down as well. At the same time though, managers and supervisors, who are themselves being pressed, may make unrealistic demands on those who report to them. As T&D professionals, how can we step forward and help our organizations make good decisions about how the work gets done? And how can we manage and design learning initiatives that are appropriate as to timing, amount, and application for the workers, giving them the best tools to do their jobs more easily and with less pressure?

Motivation

Almost everything we know about work, the workplace, and the workforce is evolving. Just as we've moved from Learning 1.0 to Learning 2.0, and from Globalization 1.0 to Globalization 3.0, we've also evolved from Motivation 2.0 (think carrots and sticks) to Motivation 3.0 (more in alignment with the 21st-century workplace). That's Dan Pink's take on this topic. Pink, author of several bestselling and cutting-edge books, has nailed it once again with his book *Drive: The Surprising Truth About What Motivates Us* (2011). In a nutshell, Pink makes the case for a new way to approach motivating workers today. He notes that while carrots and sticks—reward and penalty systems—used in the last century's workplace may have made some sense, these techniques don't work any longer.

Instead, he emphasizes that for motivation to be effective over the long term, employers need to address something much more intrinsic to a worker. Here is how he explains it:

> Motivation 3.0, the upgrade that's necessary for the smooth functioning of 21st-century business, depends on and fosters Type I [for intrinsic] behavior. Type I behavior concerns itself less with the external rewards an activity brings and more with the inherent satisfaction of the activity itself.

In other words, Pink believes that motivation can really make a difference if it is approached from our understanding of what matters most to workers as they go

WATCH! For more on Daniel Pink's fascinating explanation of Motivation 3.0 and its effects in the workplace, check out the video on YouTube: "Daniel Pink: What Really Motivates Workers."

about their work. He notes that encouraging Type I (for intrinsic) behavior is possible if the motivation approach employers take includes three elements: 1) autonomy (in what workers do, when they do it, and with whom they do it); 2) mastery; and 3) purpose. In his book, he cites case after case of organizations (using these new motivational approaches) that have outperformed their competitors (who do not look at these newer approaches to motivating their workers).

Worker Identity

Donald Super, a pioneering career development theorist of the last century, believed that an individual's self-concept is often expressed through his work, thus making the "worker role" a central one in an individual's life. Though Super's ideas may have been fit for the second half of the 20th century, and still may be true for many workers today, not all workers see themselves as workers first.

For several reasons, including layoffs, reduced resources to do one's job, burnout, and the unrelenting pace of change, many individuals have concluded that life outside of the workplace is every bit as important as life inside. Some find that leisure, community involvement, and the establishment of tighter boundaries between one's work and personal life have all become antidotes to stressful workplaces. As a result, in many instances the focus has shifted from the "worker role" to more interest and energy on activities and pursuits in non-worker roles.

Loyalty

The Herman Trend Alert recently reported on the 2011 "Employee Loyalty Declines Worldwide" survey done by Mercer. Turns out, it's not just U.S. employers lamenting a diminishing loyalty among their workers; it's happening globally. Actually, this news shouldn't come as that much of a surprise since efforts to cut budgets, find more efficiencies, and increase productivity are actions embraced by organizations across the globe.

Mindy Fox, a senior partner at Mercer quoted in the Herman Trend Alert, calls this downward movement of employee loyalty "lackluster engagement." Others might call it apathy, a lack of caring about the quality of one's work, or a general indifference toward the goals of one's employer.

What are the consequences of this diminished loyalty? Consider this: How much enthusiasm do you think learners, who are low on loyalty, will bring to your class or webinar? When you're conducting team training, how much of a team-player attitude and a collaborative mindset will they demonstrate? The Herman Trend Alert suggests that as employee loyalty plummets, companies will respond by trying to up their image and become an "Employer of Choice (2011)." But in the meantime, rather than waiting for that to happen (if it's not already part of your company's goals), what opportunities do you have to make a difference when it comes to increasing employee loyalty?

The Never-Ending Workday/Workweek

If there was ever a true norm of a 9 to 5 workplace, it doesn't show up much these days. Stretched staffs and diminished resources mean just about every worker does more, including T&D professionals. But today's workers may be carrying this newly extended workday to extremes, often because they feel they need to, if they want to hang on to their jobs. "Super commuters," who travel up to three hours one way to get to work, are on the rise. So are the numbers of people who take work home, come in extra early, and leave later than usual to get their work accomplished.

Here are some related challenges:

- **Multiple positions**—Due in large part to the recession that has left many individuals, couples, and families in more dire financial straits, people are picking up second and third jobs to make ends meet.

- **The potential dangers of "always on" connectivity**—Technology makes it easier to work from home and the chance to telecommute is making so many workers' lives easier to manage. But when do these workers feel it's OK to not answer their cell phones? When is it OK to not answer an email instantly? When does their workday end?

- **The challenge of being out of sight and therefore out of mind**—Remote workers are sometimes not kept in the loop on critical information like important deadlines. Yet, the expectation is that remote workers stay as up-to-date as their on-site colleagues.

- **The shrinking vacations**—According to a *T+D* article "Burned Out and Fed Up? Maybe All You Need Is a Break," more than 34 percent of American workers don't take all of their vacation time, and numerous workers take work with them on vacation, and respond to office emails, texts, and office phone calls while away from work (Allen, 2011).

The Worker Wish List

Workers today, regardless of sector or level of position, realize that we're still coming out of the tough times of our recent recession. Still, they are overworked, stretched thin, and hoping for some acknowledgment by their employers for all they do. If U.S.

workers could have a wish list of what they'd like to see from their employers right now, the following items would likely be at the top of that list.

Purpose

In a study featured in The Herman Trend Alert, 58 percent of U.S. workers said they'd favor joining an organization that had a clear corporate purpose, and 65 percent on average said that a company with a declared purpose would get them to go the extra mile in their jobs (2012).

Research from various sources all say the same thing: People who feel they have a purpose—something larger than themselves—live longer and are healthier.

Meaning

Teresa Amabile and Steven Kramer researched meaning and work in people's lives and reported their results in their book, *The Progress Principle* (2011). What they found isn't that surprising, yet, if ignored, it can make for a disengaged employee. The researchers found that workers truly do want to contribute —they want to make a difference.

> "Of all the events that can deeply engage people in their jobs, the single most important is making progress in meaningful work."
> —Teresa Amabile and Steven Kramer
> *McKinsey Quarterly* (2012)

More Opportunities to Learn

Other sections of this book point out the value of offering employees the chance to learn new skills. This "wish list" item shows up on several employee surveys and in conversation with workers across all functions. Most employees don't want to be bored, burned out, or to simply put in their time. They want to be challenged in meaningful ways, and T&D opportunities can provide just that.

Career Development

This, too, is an often-repeated item on many workers' wish lists. Providing career development signals to employees that their organization cares about them. In the book, *Help Them Grow or Watch Them Go*, Beverly Kaye and Julie Winkle Giulioni make the important case for ongoing career development of all employees in a tough economy (2012). When there appears to be fewer jobs inside an organization, it creates a sense of scarcity and limited options—both worrisome to employees.

Flexibility

This "wish list" item includes different types of flex programs including compressed work weeks, part-time schedules, and ad hoc telework. Interesting to note: In 2007, World atWork found that when an organization has a strong culture of flexibility, it lowers the voluntary turnover rate of workers. The Herman Trend Alert suggests there will likely be more flex programs offered by organizations worldwide, as part of their efforts to hang on to Gen Y talent (2011).

More Say in How and Where They Get Their Work Done

According to Richard Dunnett, writing in *Director* magazine, "the appetite among employees to use their personal devices for work is growing" (2012). Dunnett cites a survey done at the Unified Communications Expo that found 64 percent of employees wanted to use their own personal devices at work.

Working from home is also a much-desired perk for many. According to Global Workplace Analytics, the number of workers who currently work from home, representing 2.5 percent of the U.S. employee workforce, is 3.1 million people. The number who would like to work from home is 50 million workers (2011).

A Focus on Well-Being Instead of Balance

The term "balance" may seem like an impossibility in a 24/7 world. But that doesn't mean that it should be ignored. Gallup has been urging individuals and organizations to look at well-being as a critical factor for worker and organizational health. Tom Rath, senior scientist and advisor to Gallup notes that attention to five broad categories (Tandon, 2012) he identified is important:

- career well-being
- social well-being
- financial well-being
- physical well-being
- community well-being.

While the responsibility for one's well-being ultimately rests with the individual, workplaces can do a great deal toward taking some responsibility—through initiatives and policies to increase several areas of well-being for workers.

What You Need to Know

- Many employees are still struggling to regain their footing in a volatile, uncertain, complex, and ambiguous workplace.

- As a result, many are risk-averse and worried about the stability of their jobs.

- Workers do want to do good work, contribute, and find meaning in their jobs.

So What?

- Training and development professionals need to demonstrate an understanding of the challenges workers face as they strive to engage them in learning and performance improvement initiatives.

Why You Should Care

- Efforts at flexibility in designing programs are noticed and valued.

- Initiatives that help workers deal with stress and burnout are useful to workers.

- Additionally, programs that help workers prioritize are also quite helpful to workers doing the work of those who have been downsized.

Trend 8: New Work and the New Skills It Will Take to Do It

The comment from futurist and author Ed Gordon should get our attention and give us all a sense of the challenge we will face in the months and years to come. It's clear that huge transformations are happening across the global landscape—affecting education, business, the nonprofit and government sectors, and society in general. When it comes to the workplace,

> "Manpower has predicted that, between 2010 and 2020, 10 percent of U.S. businesses will close their doors due to the inability to fill key vacant jobs."
> —Ed Gordon
> *The Futurist* (2012)

these transformations are also changing the way we define necessary skills for today and tomorrow. They are also changing the dynamics of what work gets done, where it gets done, and by whom.

Bill Bridges, author of *Job Shift: How to Prosper in a Workplace Without Jobs*, commented back in 1995 when *Job Shift* was first published that job seekers and workers alike would need to focus their efforts on finding "the work that needs doing." In short: Old, outdated skills won't help you do the work that is currently in demand. His words are just as true today. The skill sets needed to "do the work that needs doing" keep changing.

The Skills Gap

Though the recession may be over, many of the jobs that were lost during the worst of it won't be coming back. That's because those jobs, and the skills they required, are no longer needed in today's workplace; they no longer contribute to accomplishing the work demands of today and tomorrow.

There is some confusion as to the true meaning of the phrase "skills gap," and it's hard for many to understand how there can be a true skills gap in the face of high unemployment at the same time when so many jobs go unfilled in this country. To clarify this confusion, it may be useful to start with a clear definition. In 2012, ASTD published a whitepaper on this topic: *Bridging the Skills Gap: Help Wanted, Skills Lacking: Why the Mismatch in Today's Economy?* In this important paper:

> ASTD defines a skills gap as a significant gap between an organization's current capabilities and the skills it needs to achieve its goals. It is the point at which an organization can no longer grow or remain competitive because it cannot fill critical jobs with employees who have the right knowledge, skills, and abilities.

This definition helps us to see the true predicament we're facing. Individuals, as well as states, regions, and many sectors of the economy, are experiencing a skills gap. A job seeker looking for work as an auto mechanic without the latest training to fix and maintain cars built with advanced technologies, fuel-injection systems, and advanced multimedia control systems will have a difficult time finding work. So will HVAC (heating, ventilation, and air conditioning) technicians, whose education ended five years ago, and they haven't upgraded their skills since then. And so will the trainer, who may be great at classroom training, but not so cutting-edge when it comes to e-learning skills and the ability to convert in-person training into engaging e-learning formats.

As T&D professionals, we must take this skills gap into consideration as we help our organizations develop a strategy to identify needs both for the short and long term. We certainly cannot ignore the issue and hope that somehow new and current workers will continue to show up "workplace ready" and qualified, no matter what the workplace's evolving skill set demands may look like. They won't. Helping our employer address the skills gap will make a difference in the trajectory of our own career—and the success of the job seekers, students, workers, and organizations we serve.

Globalization and the Skills Gap

Talent has been redistributed around the world. According to some recent reports, over the next decade, India and China will have a surplus of talent, while regions like the U.S., much of Europe, and Japan may have a deficit. Bottom line—globalization affects the skills gap in several ways:

- Students who come to the U.S. for education may find more opportunities back in their home countries, once they've graduated.

- More talent is being "home-grown."

- Many countries have an aging population.

- In some countries, government may take a more active role to provide its citizens with more access to education for emerging in-demand skills.

LISTEN! For more on the talent shortage issue, listen to the audio from the Executive Search Blog, "The Battle for the Best—Globalization and the Talent Shortage."

But Is There Really a Skills Gap?

The answer to that question is…it depends. In an *HBR* blog post, Matt Ferguson, CEO of CareerBuilder, explains part of the problem that contributes to this confusion. He suggests that we are "experiencing the symptoms of a multi-speed labor market." He goes on to explain the implications: "This means job sectors that require highly educated workers are recovering fast, while growth in other areas will likely remain stagnant until consumer demand begins to rise. And the skills required to fill many of the jobs returning first in the recovery—namely in engineering, IT, and healthcare—do not match the skills of Americans most needing work" (2011). Ferguson goes on to suggest that companies can take the initiative to retrain in such situations.

Bridging the Skills Gap

Dr. John Sullivan, recognized as a thought leader in the field of human resources and talent management, notes that "training and development must create the capability to prepare employees and managers to identify and effectively handle previously unknown problems." He suggests the need for rapid learning: "systems to increase the speed of individual and organizational learning" and more fluid job descriptions: "continually evolving job descriptions and hiring standards that reflect the continually changing work" (2012).

The Talent Mismatch

Justin Ashton, cofounder of XL Hybrids, a Boston-based developer of technology that converts vehicles to hybrids, offers an example of a talent-mismatch problem he is facing. Mr. Ashton actively tries to hire veterans. As he puts it: "Vets bring a lot to the table. But the jobs that are open are more technical than they were 10 years ago, and there is a mismatch in skills." He recommends that those working with vets help them secure jobs and provide more up-to-date training. He notes: "It is a very competitive job market, and they [veterans] are competing against people with more focused skills" (Quittner, 2013).

This same scenario is being played out across the country as long-term unemployed people have lost their ability to stay current and workers in dwindling job sectors find themselves skilled in jobs that are no longer in demand.

Another piece of the skills-gap puzzle that needs to be addressed: the broken leadership pipeline. Though many companies are aware of their challenge to pay more attention to their succession-planning process, not enough are working to identify potential leaders to fill future leadership roles. They aren't giving these employees the skills they need to step into leadership positions in the future.

The Education-to-Employment Conundrum

There is often a disconnect for students when they graduate from high school or college and find that they don't have the skills the employer is looking for. This disturbing issue continues to hold back young adults and holds back companies who can't find graduates who fit their needs. McKinsey & Company has issued a powerful report on this issue: *Education to Employment: Designing a System That Works* (2012).

 WATCH! This important McKinsey research project is accessible at http://mckinseyonsociety.com/. View the video first, then access the full report.

In their study of the education-to-employment journey that young adults make, they identified several challenges. Among them:

- Educators, employers, and youth have "different understandings of the same situation." The study found that fewer than 50 percent of youth and employers believe that new graduates are adequately prepared for entry-level positions, while 72 percent of educational providers believe they are.

- The same thing held true when they looked at education and the problem of students dropping out. More than one-third of educational providers believe that students drop out because their course of study is too hard; yet only 9 percent of students say this is the case.

The authors of the McKinsey study believe the problem is a lack of engagement between the three groups; not enough educators and employers work together to solve the issue; and not enough youth truly understand which disciplines might provide them with the best chances of successfully applying for and accepting good paying jobs (2012).

Unless this problem is addressed by employers and educational institutions working together, it does not seem likely that today's young adults will be any better prepared to get those higher paying in-demand jobs.

Responses to the Skills Shortage Warning

Accenture, a global management consultancy organization, looked into the skills gap (2011) through an online survey and found that although workers have the motivation to gain critical skills and knowledge, they lack the necessary support to do so (Garff, 2012).

In their study, Accenture made recommendations to companies who are trying to deal with the skills gap they are experiencing, including ones that tie closely to the work that T&D professionals can do in their organizations:

- Seek to discover the untapped talent in your organization.

- Focus on the basic job requirements, allowing for greater hiring flexibility by looking for growth and development potential in candidates.

- Create an environment for learning that allows employees to work on developing skills on a regular basis.

- Redefine responsibilities in a way that highlights talents and existing skills.

- Clearly define skill requirements for employees, as well as educational institutions and the broader community.

GOOD TO KNOW! For a look at the full Accenture Skills Gap Study, search for "Accenture Study Finds U.S. Workers Under Pressure to Improve Skills, But Need More Support From Employers."

Future Work Skills for Today's Workers

Apollo Research Institute conducted a study to determine which skills will be most important in the years ahead, given all the complexity and continual change we'll be facing.

Here is their list of the top six "Future Work Skills 2020":

- **Virtual Collaboration:** "The ability to work productively, drive engagement, and demonstrate presence as a member of a virtual team…"

- **Design Mindset:** "The ability to represent and develop tasks and work processes for desired outcomes that will allow humans to design their world…"

- **Computational Thinking:** "The ability to translate vast amounts of data into abstract concepts and to understand data-based reasoning…"

- **New Media Literacy:** The ability to "critically assess and develop content in new media forms and…leverage new media to communicate persuasively…"

- **Novel and Adaptive Thinking:** The ability to "be proficient at going beyond role or rule-based solutions to respond quickly and adaptively to unfamiliar circumstances."

- **Transdisciplinarity:** "The ability to integrate different sets of knowledge and fluency across multiple disciplines…" (Davis, Fidler, and Gorbis, 2011).

GOOD TO KNOW! For a look at their full report, search for Apollo Research Institute's "Future Work Skills 2020."

You may notice that several of the skills from the list you just read involved "soft skills." The need for both soft and hard skills is critical—regardless of the advances that come from technology. Washington D.C.-based futurist Jennifer Jarratt said many years ago that one of the most critical skills a potential employee needs to demonstrate is "the ability to play well with others." Obviously, this skill will continue to be of high importance in our workplace going forward.

What You Need to Know

- In the words of Marshall Goldsmith's 2007 book, *What Got You Here Won't Get You There!,* the skills that workers counted on to keep them employed aren't necessarily ones that they'll need in the future.

- New work will require new skills—yet, many workers and job seekers have not made the connection between "new work" and how that will affect them.

So What?

- To best help our organizations and employees, training and development professionals need to be able to see the need for new skills and embrace new ways of learning to be successful going forward.

Why You Should Care

- You, as a T&D professional, can play a key role here: You can take the lead in helping organizations design learning strategies to get current employees up-skilled and reskilled; and you can help plan for future organizational needs, when it comes to helping them remain competitive.

Chapter 2

Introducing the ASTD 2013 Competency Model

Master Key Foundational Competencies and Polish Your Areas of Expertise

After reading through the key trends listed in chapter 1 that are certain to affect you, your profession, and the people and organizations you work with, it's likely you're asking yourself: "Now what?" You've reviewed the details of each trend and you "get it" in terms of knowing their importance in the current and future workplace. But you may still be wondering how your heightened awareness and increased knowledge of these trends can make a difference in your own career growth.

More specifically, you may be thinking:

- How can I use my knowledge of these eight trends to add more value to my own portfolio of skills?

- What are the key skill sets I need to demonstrate to best leverage my knowledge of these trends?

- How can I determine my own optimal career path within an ever-changing and highly demanding workplace where learning has become so crucial?

- Where do I look for guidance on building a solid career development plan for myself?

If any or all of these questions are on your mind, you've come to exactly the right place.

The 2013 ASTD Competency Model

The *ASTD Competency Study: The Training & Development Profession Redefined*, released earlier this year, offers a comprehensive, up-to-date framework and a clear depiction of the themes and actions that are critical for success in the T&D field today and tomorrow. The 2013 Model™ represents the latest thinking and showcases the most important areas that professionals in the field need to be aware of and act on, if we want to be effective and deliver the most value to those with whom we work.

For a summary of the latest Model, be sure to read: "Training and Development Competencies Redefined to Create Competitive Advantage" by Justin Arneson, William Rothwell, and Jennifer Naughton in the January, 2013 issue of *T+D*. And don't miss the sidebar in that same article: "The Wake-Up Call." The article does an outstanding job of explaining the evolution of the ASTD Model, and it offers tools to help you leverage the Model for your own career growth and professional development.

The Value of a Competency Model in Guiding Your Own Career

One of the key challenges we all face today within our field is determining what is most important for us to know to remain relevant and stay on our cutting edge. Just like everyone else, we're inundated with an increasing amount of information coming from dozens of reliable sources. So what do we pay attention to? How do we sift through all the journal articles, websites, books, and communities of practice to ferret out the most essential information we need to know to be effective? That is where a competency model can help.

As authors Arneson, Rothwell, and Naughton point out:

> Competencies are important for defining any profession. They provide a common language for describing performance and a guide for identifying the knowledge, skills, and behaviors that practitioners need to be successful performers (2013).

The ASTD Competency Model, derived from an extensive research study (and explained in the *ASTD Competency Study* book), offers you a tool to help you grow your career, spot gaps in your own experience and performance, and support your efforts to deepen your expertise. It won't do the work for you, but it certainly can make it easier for you to choose the areas you want to focus on as you develop your career.

Before we go any further, it may be helpful to take a step back and look more closely at just what a competency is and how it can be useful to your professional growth. According to authors William Rothwell and James Graber in their book, *Competency-Based Training Basics*, the term *competency:*

> …refers to any characteristics of an individual performer that lead to acceptable or outstanding performance. Competencies may include technical skills, level of motivation, personality traits, awareness of bodies of knowledge, or just about anything else that can assist in producing results. Competencies are the domain of individuals; thus, it is important to remember that analysis of successful performers is one of the best ways to isolate and identify qualities that make some people more successful than others (2010).

So with the knowledge that competencies can be used to identify and measure performance, you can better understand how the Model can help you. The ASTD Model offers you guidance in several ways:

- It provides an overview of topics that represent essential, need-to-know areas, which are critical for understanding the complexities of today's workplace and the major role that learning now plays within it.

- It delineates specific actions you need to take if you want to make a difference and distinguish yourself as a true professional.

- The graphic used to depict the Model (see page 62) shows how the different elements (Foundational Competencies and Areas of Expertise—AOEs) support one another and contribute to the Model's overall goal of using characteristics and proficiencies that T&D professionals must demonstrate to be successful in the current business environment.

- It serves as a handy job aid—a visual reminder of all the components that link the various roles and actions important to our field.

Look over the ASTD 2013 Competency Model before reading any further in this chapter. If you understand the structure of the Model, it can help you get an idea of where you stand currently compared to the most important themes and actions necessary for success in our field.

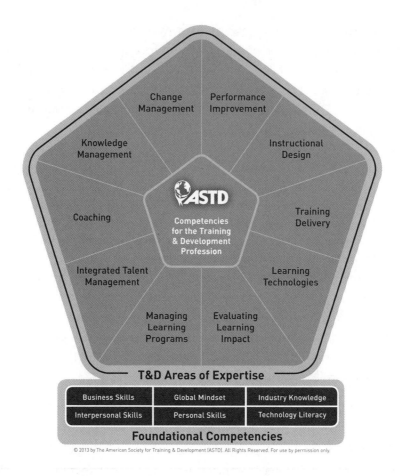

The Six Foundational Competencies

The six Foundational Competencies of the ASTD Competency Model are keys to your success. They represent the critical, bedrock areas that you need to master in order to be seen as savvy and relevant by those you work with. As you review them, you'll notice that they are not specific to the training and development field. However, they are essential business-related skills that you must have to truly understand your organization's needs and to be able to affect your organization's overall effectiveness and success.

The Foundational Competencies include:

1. Business Skills:
- Analyzing Needs and Proposing Solutions: identifies and understands business issues and client needs, problems, and opportunities and uses this knowledge to design effective approaches for learning opportunities.

- Applying Business Skills: understands the organization's business strategies, key metrics, and financial goals.

- Driving Results: identifies opportunities for improvement and sets well-defined goals realted to learning and development solutions.

- Planning and Implementing Assignments: develops action plans and completes assignments to ensure achievement of learning and development goals.

- Thinking Strategically: understands internal and external factors that affect learning and development inside organizations and uses that knowledge to create learning and development strategies.

- Applying Innovation: uses new resources, methods, tools, or content to advance learning and development and applies existing techniques in new ways.

2. **Global Mindset:** appreciates and leverages the capabilities and ideas of all individuals and works effectively with individuals across generational, cultural, ability, and learning style backgrounds and experiences to benefit them and to build a robust, inclusive workforce within their organization.

3. **Industry Knowledge:** scans and assesses information on current and emerging trends in the learning and development industry; maintains knowledge of other industries, as appropriate.

4. **Interpersonal Skills:**
   - Building Trust: interacts with others in ways that give them confidence in one's intentions.

   - Communicating Effectively: expresses thoughts, feelings, and ideas in a clear, concise, and compelling manner in both individual and group situations.

   - Influencing Stakeholders: sells the value of learning or the recommended solution as a way of improving an organization's performance, and gains commitment across the organization.

   - Networking and Partnering: develops and uses a network of collaborative relationships inside and outside the organization to facilitate accomplishment of business results.

   - Emotional Intelligence: perceives the emotional state of one's own self and others accurately and uses this information to guide effective decision making and build positive work relationships.

5. **Personal Skills:**
   - Demonstrating Adaptability: maintains effectiveness when experiencing major changes in work tasks, the work environment, or conditions affecting the

organization, while remaining open to new possibilities and effectively adjusting to work within new work structures.

- Modeling Personal Development: actively identifies new learning opportunities, takes advantage of them, and applies them within one's work setting.

6. Technology Literacy: demonstrates an awareness of and comfort with existing, new, and emerging technologies and identifies opportunities to leverage new technology to accomplish learning tasks and achieve business goals.

The Areas of Expertise—10 Ways to Demonstrate Your Capabilities

While the Foundational Competencies are meant to ensure a solid base of the business-related skills that are most needed, the Areas of Expertise (AOEs) represent the functional T&D competencies that are needed by professionals in our field. The 10 AOEs listed below (from the 2013 *ASTD Competency Study* book) represent "a variety of specialized knowledge, skills, abilities, and other characteristics that may be needed by T&D professionals" (Arneson, Rothwell, & Naughton, *T+D*, 2013).

As you review these 10 AOEs, you'll see that they represent a wide range of specialized knowledge and actions, and you'll also notice that these 10 areas are more specific to the T&D field. The degree of skill and expertise will vary, depending on your amount of time in the field or the type of career you aspire to. You may be new to the field; if so, your degree of skill in any of the AOEs would probably be less than that of a T&D professional who has been growing a particular cluster of AOEs for more than 10 years. As you review these 10 areas, consider where you are now and what function(s) you'd like to be moving toward in the future.

Remember, it is not necessary to have expertise in all 10 of these areas. The ones that will be most important to you—the ones you will want to pay most attention to—depend on your current role in your organization and your own career aspirations as you look forward. Here is a complete listing of all the latest Areas of Expertise. For a more in-depth look, review the latest competency study book.

Areas of Expertise
1. **Performance Improvement:** Applying a systematic process of discovering and analyzing human performance gaps.
2. **Instructional Design:** Designing, creating, and developing informal and formal learning solutions to meet organizational needs by using appropriate strategy, methodologies, and technologies.

3. **Training Delivery:** Delivering informal and formal learning solutions that engage the learner and produce desired outcomes; and ensuring that the learning is made available in effective platforms and delivered in a timely and effective manner.

4. **Learning Technologies:** Identifying, selecting, and applying various learning technologies.

5. **Evaluating Learning Impact:** Gathering, organizing, analyzing, and presenting information on the impact of learning solutions and using learning metrics and analytics to inform organizational decision making.

6. **Managing Learning Programs:** Providing leadership to execute the organization's strategy; planning, monitoring, and adjusting learning and development projects or activities.

7. **Integrated Talent Management:** Building an organization's culture, engagement, capability, and capacity through implementation and integration of talent acquisition, employee development, retention, and deployment processes.

8. **Coaching:** Using an interactive process to help individuals develop rapidly and produce results.

9. **Knowledge Management:** Capturing, distributing, and archiving intellectual capital.

10. **Change Management:** Applying structured approaches to shift individuals, teams, and organizations from a current state to a desired state.

GOOD TO KNOW! There are now free and very low-cost online services that let e-learning developers see what works and what doesn't. Use these web analytics software tools to refine your design to make your e-learning more user-friendly, engaging, and helpful to learners. Some of these tools include: Google Analytics (www.google.com/analytics), Crazy Egg (http://crazyegg.com), and Mint (www.haveamint.com).

Tools to Help You Navigate Your Career

Now that you have a better idea of the key trends and the competencies and skills you will need to shape your career path going forward, you can take advantage of the Career Navigator, a career resource tool on the ASTD website (if you are an ASTD member). Here is a brief overview of this tool, taken from the Career Navigator webpage:

The ASTD Career Navigator will help you explore the career roles you can aspire to, the skills necessary to function effectively in each role, and the resources that are available to help build necessary skills. Based on the 2013 ASTD Competency Model, the Career Navigator will allow you to assess your current skills, and after completing the tool you will receive a report that shows you how you rate yourself against the target proficiencies needed in that position. Training activities will then be recommended to close any proficiency gaps.

GOOD TO KNOW! You may want to visit the Career Navigator page now, to familiarize yourself with it and then return to it again, once you've read through section II of this book. You can access the Career Navigator page by going to: www.astd.org/Careernavigator (available to ASTD members only).

GOOD TO KNOW! Another great resource for you, as you build your career path in the training and development field, is the Career Development Community of Practice section of the ASTD website. Within that community, you'll find resources to help you at every stage of your career, from beginning in the field to becoming an expert within your particular area of interest. Learn more at astd.org.

Alignment Matters

Training events and learning initiatives have always focused on relevancy and impact on a company's bottom line. But today, the challenges are even greater to get the most from any type of learning initiative, from onboarding new employees, to capturing the knowledge of retiring workers. No initiative can be "stand-alone" and every initiative needs to align with the business needs of the organization.

We are seeing huge changes in our workplace, especially those brought on by advances in learning technologies and an increased focus on innovation. As a result, most of us feel an increased pressure to help organizations further advance their goals and affect their bottom line. So it is imperative that T&D professionals make certain that whatever area of expertise we're utilizing (designing, facilitating, implementing, or managing the learning function), we are doing so in line with our organization's top priorities.

Think Multiple Paths to Excel in Work That Matters

Beverly Kaye wrote a book in the early 1980s, *Up Is Not the Only Way*, which has become timeless. Of course the workplace has changed significantly since then, and so have the challenges within it. But her words of advice for how to seek career opportunities are just as true today as when she first wrote them. The challenge, as she wrote about recently in a *T+D* article, is to "redefine career success to include more than just traditional vertical moves" (2012). While this is an important strategy for organizations and employees, it's also important for you, as a T&D professional. Among her suggestions for you to consider: lateral moves, growing in place, moving up, investigating possibilities, moving down or back, and moving out.

Beyond these suggestions, do not limit yourself to one goal. Once you've identified where and how you want to make a difference professionally, you can begin to consider all the different types of positions that will let you contribute in ways that appeal to you. Section II of this book will help you do just that.

Distinguish Yourself and Flourish in Your Field

This is a very exciting and transformational time to be part of the training industry. As employees become more resourceful in fulfilling their own learning needs, the focus on comprehensive course development will probably decrease. In its place, the learning and development professional will likely take on a role that supports and enables learning. This could encompass roles, such as managing communities of practice, helping staff create their own personal learning environments, and setting up wikis to capture organizational knowledge.

Connie Malamed, Publisher of The E-Learning Coach website

It's quite likely that you were drawn to this book—and you are reading it right now—because you're committed to the T&D field and to your own career growth and professional development.

It is also likely that, as an aspiring or experienced professional, you are serious about making a difference, you understand the need to update your skills and be more aware of the latest workplace trends, and you want to continue to hone your edge to distinguish yourself. While you value the education, training, and experience you already have, you probably recognize that there will always be a learning curve to master. But because you want to contribute to the field and make a difference, it's likely you see these learning curves as opportunities to grow and contribute rather than as "requirements" you must adhere to if you want to remain employable.

Put the Trends and the Model Together

While chapter 2 presented the ASTD 2013 Competency Model and suggested a wide range of opportunities to grow and deepen your skill sets, chapter 3 focuses on the **why** and **how** of distinguishing yourself as a savvy professional in the T&D field.

In many ways, the trends you read about in chapter 1 have raised the bar for those of us in the training and development field. It's not enough to know the latest learning-related technologies, or to master an instructional design process, or even to create a coaching initiative. These skills are all great, but alone, they are not enough.

We must take what we **know** and **leverage** it to help our organization, employees, or job seekers to succeed. For example, to deliver value, we must:

- know which technologies to use **and** why they are the best ones for a particular learning initiative

- understand the principles of engagement **and** then use the appropriate engagement tools to reach different segments of our very diverse workforce to gain buy-in, improve performance, or increase productivity across the organization

- recognize the strengths and skill sets of the employees we work with **and** find ways those employees can use more of their strengths to benefit themselves and their employers.

In other words, to succeed as a T&D professional today, we must put what we know to work:

- to align employee and employer objectives

- to facilitate all employees' abilities to demonstrate and contribute their strengths

- to make a bottom-line difference to the organizations we serve.

What Is Your Value Proposition?

Maybe this term is already one you're familiar with—or maybe you're thinking that "value proposition" is what marketers need to come up with to help their organizations sell a product or skill. The truth is, every employee and job seeker today needs to have a personal value proposition (PVP). Organizations are looking for workers who "add value" to their bottom line—and that is true for any type of organization you can think of—because it's not enough to show up with the same skills as the 20 (or more) people applying for the same job. If you're already employed, it's not enough to go into work each day thinking that what got you hired is enough to keep you employed.

> "If you have a job where someone tells you what to do next, you've just given up the chance to create value."
>
> —Seth Godin
> author of *Linchpin: Are You Indispensable?*

You offer talent to your boss, your team, or to a potential employer. It is your uniqueness and your ability to stand out and make the case for the value you can offer that will get you closer to the position you are applying for or the promotion you seek.

Mind Tools describes a value proposition as "a short statement that clearly communicates the benefits that your potential client gets by using your product, service, or idea" (2013). A value proposition does the same thing for you—it lets you communicate what it is that you, as a T&D professional, can offer to an employer. Mind Tools notes that "the idea is to help them [your prospective employer] see the specific value your offer brings to them."

 GOOD TO KNOW! Here are some ideas from www.mindtools.com to help you build your own PVP.

Here are some suggestions from Mind Tools, combined with reflections on how these suggestions can be relevant to T&D professionals.

- Know your customer/potential employer/head of a project you want to be part of (and also know the trends you read about earlier so you can relate these trends and your skills to meet the need of your customer).

- Know your products, service, or idea. What specifically do you have to offer? Consider which AOEs represent your areas of strength.

- Know your competitors. You may not know everyone who is applying for the promotion or position you seek, but you can get an idea of the likely level of skills of others who are applying by reviewing the job announcement, and through your social media connections, you may get an idea of who has held the position before, or who excels in the kind of work you're seeking. Use this information to benchmark your own skills.

- Distill the customer-oriented proposition. Try looking at the situation from the employer's perspective: (What unique combination of skills, competencies, and AOEs do you, as a T&D professional, have that would solve the employer's problem or contribute to that company's growth and success?)

Personal Branding Is a Differentiator

> "Personal branding is about finding your voice, taking ownership of your career path, and feeling empowered in what you contribute to the world. Personal branding supports and enhances your work as a training and development professional by identifying what makes you unique and communicates your individuality to the people who need to know about you. Your personal brand is your reputation and helps you navigate the direction of your life so that you can live your best self."
>
> —Susan Chritton
> author of *Personal Branding for Dummies*

At its simplest, your "brand" represents how you are perceived by others. It is the impression that others get from seeing how you behave and noticing how you present yourself. It is much more than a style of dress, a particular degree or credential, or the associations you belong to—it is all of these things and more—mainly it is the unique "stamp" you put on everything you say or do. Because no one will do things and present themselves in exactly the same way that you do, your uniqueness is what people notice.

If you're one of those people who wonder if "branding" is just the latest buzzword that will fade by tomorrow, consider this: Our economy is on its way to recovery and it's likely that more professionals across every field (including ours) will be looking for new opportunities. Even those who aren't looking for new jobs will likely be looking for ways to position themselves for promotions or key assignments inside their organizations. That is what savvy careerists do.

With these workplace realities in mind, and with the high probability that you, too, want to advance your own career in some way, ask yourself if you are doing all you can to distinguish yourself as a forward-thinking (and acting) professional.

Personal branding is a tool that enables you to do just that: Distinguish yourself. Personal branding lets others know more about you and more about the way you approach your work; it helps others make a better decision when they are looking for expertise to solve their problems. We buy products and services we trust. We continue to use them because we know who or what they represent—we can count on them—and that is why we choose them over their competitors.

Contrary to what some mistakenly believe about branding, it's not about hype or inauthentic self-promotion. Personal branding is about finding ways to let others know who you are, what you are best at, and how you are unique and different from others with a similar background or experience. Four people may apply for the same position of trainer, but each of the four will approach the task in different ways, offer different strengths, and make an impact in their own particular way.

Your job is to make certain everyone knows in what ways you are outstanding and what unique qualities you can contribute to the task or to the organization. To become more acquainted with branding, look at the resources in the back of this book and also check out the suggested link here.

LISTEN! Check out this link to listen to a number of podcasts and videos on the topic of branding: www.personalbranding.tv/

Follow the Advice of Seth, Marcus, and Tom

Each of the individuals mentioned in this section are well-known for their perspective on changes in the workplace, the importance of skills, and the value of strengths. Together, they all make a strong case for identifying, honoring, and demonstrating our strengths to make a difference in the workplace.

Seth Godin wants you to be a linchpin. In his book *Linchpin: Are You Indispensable?*, he makes the important case for making yourself indispensable by choosing to do things differently than those who simply "show up" for work each day and bring none of their best work or their best selves with them. Godin suggests that we all have a choice: either be just like everyone else (or like the 50 other people who are after the same job you are), or make a difference (2010).

Consider this scenario that Godin uses to illustrate how most people seek a job, a promotion, or a coveted assignment:

> Your résumé sits in a stack of plenty of other résumés, each striving to fit in and meet the requirements. Your cubicle is next to the other cubes, much like each other. Your business card and suit and approach to problems—all designed to fit in. You keep your head down and work hard and hope you get picked (2010).

While that may be the usual route for many people, it's not likely to be the approach that will get you noticed. Godin suggests there is another approach to consider: Become a linchpin. Here is his description of a linchpin: "The linchpin is an individual who can walk into chaos and create order, someone who can invent, connect, create, and make things happen. Every worthwhile institution has indispensable people who make differences like these" (2010).

How can pursuing the linchpin route benefit you in your career? You may be thinking that the definition of linchpin doesn't describe you. You don't invent new things everyday—and you don't necessarily turn workplace chaos into order in the blink of an eye. But that is not what Godin is suggesting. He is suggesting that, by bringing to work your finest talents and engagement, you make a difference. And the fastest route to making a difference as a T&D professional is to first master the Foundational Competencies mentioned in the previous chapter. Then, go on to identify the AOEs that will both meet the requirements for the positions you aspire to and also bring out your finest talents and expertise. Seth Godin's message to us here: We can best become linchpins when we are honing and demonstrating our strengths.

Marcus Buckingham, founder of The Marcus Buckingham Company (TMBC), author, and consultant, has devoted several years to researching and identifying individual and organizational strengths. In his recent book *StandOut* (2011), he focuses on helping individuals identify and leverage their cutting-edge strengths. He also makes the case for innovation—and its necessity in today's workplace.

Innovation isn't just a must-have for organizations. Innovation is a must-have for your own career as well. Chances are good that if you're an experienced trainer, you've identified the "secret sauce" to keep your participants engaged. If you're an executive coach, you have some particular questions you like to ask that encourage your clients to open up or stretch their limits. These actions represent innovation—using your own particular strengths and taking them a step further to really make a difference. As a T&D professional, have you taken the time to think through the particular way that you succeed? Do you know what it is that gains you high marks for the work you do—and for how you do it?

Tom Rath, author of *Strengths Finder 2.0* (2007), has spent years working with his team at Gallup to develop and refine tools to help individuals identify their strengths and put them to use. One of the powerful findings of their studies is that workers who can focus on their strengths are much more engaged in their jobs, and are more likely to experience a higher quality of life, overall. That's fantastic news that you can use in your own career growth.

Why not use the information about emerging trends you've learned here, together with the latest competencies and AOEs—and the powerful exercises you'll find in section II—to identify your strengths, your skills gaps, and the areas in which you want to excel? You have the tools you need to move your career ahead. May your future be full of opportunities to succeed in the training and development field.

Chapter 4

Leverage Your Full Spectrum of Opportunities

Capitalize on Your Strengths, on or off the Traditional Career Path

ere's a question worth pondering before you go any further. Are you prepared to apply the latest information available on emerging trends, the needs of your learners, and the critical competencies presented in the previous chapters, to become even more savvy and on target in your own work? If you are—and if you're ready to invest time and effort into digging even deeper in the areas most relevant and interesting to you—congratulations! You're setting yourself up for taking advantage of a much wider array of career opportunities.

Welcome to YOYO Land

Helen Harkness, futurist, author, and career coach, was spot on when she introduced the term "YOYO land" in an article (2008). Dr. Harkness used the acronym to alert us all to the fact that we are working in a world where **Y**ou're **O**n **Y**our **O**wn. Support, encouragement, and guidance may come from a trusted advisor or your boss or your organization—but it isn't a wise idea to sit around waiting for someone to tap you on the shoulder and show you the golden path to career success.

Instead, the smart thing to do is take control of your own career, be mindful about it, making a plan—while still being flexible enough to entertain multiple strategies to move you in the direction of career satisfaction, inside or outside the traditional path.

Forget the Ladder—Embrace the Lattice

If you happened to see the cover of *Businessweek* magazine in October, 2009, you may have been a bit curious about what you saw. Regardless of your age or career stage or status, the picture got the attention of all of us who are interested in career progression.

The cover of the magazine showed a very tall, narrow ladder with several rungs missing or broken. The message in the cover story was that those between the ages of 16 and 24 have unemployment rates that are significantly higher than those born into other generations. Those in the so-called lost generation are likely to struggle with pursuing their career path and are not likely to be able to "climb" the traditional career ladder to advancement.

 WATCH! For more about the lost generation's work and career-related challenges, check out the Bloomberg Businessweek video titled "The `Lost Generation': Young and Underemployed."

While the "broken career ladder" story focused on the Millennial generation, the article's message is a cautionary tale for all those seeking employment and advancement. The truth is: that old career ladder is a remnant of the last century.

What is one of the first things you would notice if you looked at a ladder? Chances are good you would notice that there's only one way up or down. If you wanted to reach the upper rungs, unless you wanted to crawl on the backs of those ahead of you, you would have to wait your turn till the rung above you became available. And, if your ladder had rungs missing, you would have to take precarious giant steps upward, not knowing for sure if you would safely make it to the next one up.

Instead of a ladder, consider a lattice. If you take the lattice structure, and combine it with new ideas about career progression, you have a **career lattice**. Joanne Cleaver, author of *The Career Lattice*, defines this emerging model of career-thinking this way: "A career lattice is a diagonal framework that braids lateral experiences, adjacent skill acquisition, and peer networking to move employees to any of a variety of positions for which they have become qualified" (2012). Ms. Cleaver believes that one's ability to "lattice" across, up, and down different positions will be a critical skill in the years to come.

In the second section of this book, you'll get more details about how you can use career latticing to make your own career moves.

The Power and the Limitations of Job Titles

Still stuck thinking of yourself as "just" a trainer? Or "just" an instructional designer? Or a learning manager? Labeling yourself by one job title is a holdover from the 20th century. To get yourself closer to today's "job title" thinking, consider the term coined by Marci Alboher and used in the title of her 2007 book: *One Person/Multiple Careers: The Original Guide to the Slash Career*. The implication behind her title? Savvy careerists don't limit themselves to one job title; in fact, most of us contribute to our current job in multiple ways, or we contribute to multiple jobs (our day job and our weekend or part-time employment endeavors) by using more than one strength.

While there are limitations to thinking only of job titles—especially just one job title—titles do serve a useful purpose. If you make it a point to keep up with the latest job titles and projected "job titles of the future," as well as the upticks in occupations that are growing in number, you can use job titles to stay ahead of the curve. You can also search online for new and emerging job titles and careers that give you important information of what the "work that needs doing" will be and where this work might be located (by industry sector, geography, and skills needed).

GOOD TO KNOW! Want a couple ideas for becoming more job title savvy? Check out the "You're a What?" feature of the Occupational Outlook Quarterly, as well as other great information on this site for new and emerging jobs. (www.bls.gov/opub/ooq/home.htm) Or use your favorite search engine to scan what's next for jobs by searching a term like "job titles of the future" to see some amazing (as well as some very different) descriptors that go far beyond job titles we're accustomed to seeing.

Meet Some T&D Professionals

This next section gives you a closer look at the career paths, career concerns, and career questions of some T&D professionals as they consider a job search, promotion campaign, or career restart (later in their careers).

> "Jobs may come and jobs may go but your career belongs to you."
>
> —Eunice Azzani
> Founder and Partner, Azzani Search Consultants

The remainder of this chapter introduces you to four individuals, each facing a different career decision point. Each individual has T&D experience, training-related education, or both. Each one is considering options for what's next career-wise. You'll get to know these people much better in the second section of this book, as they apply the information you've learned in this first section to their own lives and as their career-related efforts and activities are highlighted.

Meet Lakshmi

Lakshmi, 23, has just graduated from college with a BS in training and development and a concentration in instructional design. She knows that T&D is the place she wants to be—but she's a bit clueless on how to move toward identifying and pursuing the right career opportunities for herself. She's also unsure about where to look: Should she limit her search locally to her home state of Illinois, or should she consider a wider range of opportunities?

Lakshmi has always been interested in teaching and training, and she volunteered as a tutor during her undergraduate days. She completed two internships in her junior and senior years of college. The first internship let her gain experience in the HR department of a high-tech company, where she participated in the orientation and onboarding process of new employees.

Her second internship was at a professional association where she had the chance to assist in designing online professional development courses for the association's membership. Lakshmi loved both internships and found a real passion for creating online programs that engaged her audience.

One of her challenges is that while she worked so hard at her courses and internships, she hasn't taken much time to establish connections with any companies or professionals who are already in the field beyond those she met through her internships.

Currently, she's most excited about how technology enables learning to happen in so many different ways. In her spare time, Lakshmi devours anything she can read, watch, or listen to that's related to technology and learning; she regularly scours the latest publications in her local bookstore. She faithfully checks her favorite tech-related blogs for news of the latest tech trends, and tries out any new webinar or app so she can advance her technological skills, especially those related to learning.

Her friends tease her about her obsession with anything tech-related, but she is always the first one they ask when they're trying to learn how to use a new app or when they are getting ready to make a new tech purchase. When Lakshmi isn't deep in learning the latest tech trends, she enjoys her "hobby" of building her language skills; while she's fluent in two languages at the moment, she really wants to increase her fluency in other languages. Currently she's teaching herself French (with the help of an online program and a good friend). Next, she wants to move her Spanish skills up from just basic comprehension to more of a conversational competency level.

While she is savvy about many facets of online learning and social media, Lakshmi is also rather shy about sharing her own areas of expertise (she feels she is young and may not be seen as knowing enough yet to be taken seriously by employers).

Meet Ric

He's 43, says he wants to keep growing, but doesn't know what else or where else he can use his skills. Ric graduated more than 20 years ago with a bachelor's degree in business administration and a concentration in human resource management. As a first-generation college student, Ric is proud of his academic accomplishments and likes to serve as a role model for others in his community who are considering attending college.

After an initial stint in the benefits office of HR administration at a law firm, he chose to make a lateral move to the Leadership Development Program Initiative at his organization, where he got to coordinate executive development efforts, including establishing a mentoring program, and partnering with a couple local colleges to initiate an internship program for underrepresented minorities.

Ric has become the go-to person in his company for advice on how to encourage and prepare early career employees for taking on leadership roles. Midlevel managers, in particular, seek him out for help on working with their direct reports.

Though Ric continues to enjoy his work and knows he's made a significant contribution to his organization, he's noticed he has a sense of burnout lately. He still performs well in his work, continues to be sought out for his opinion, and continues to stay current on leadership-related trends and issues. He just doesn't get very excited about these topics anymore. In addition, he knows that he's near the top of his opportunities for promotion: His company doesn't have much room for advancement in his particular area of expertise beyond the level he's at right now.

As a result, Ric has begun to question his future direction—though he believes in what his organization is doing, he sometimes wonders what he might accomplish in another work setting where he might feel more challenged by new projects or new areas where he can capitalize on his expertise.

In addition to his work role, Ric is quite active in his community, including serving on his city's leadership initiative, in which he gets to speak to local high school and college students about developing leadership skills. He's also active in his kids' athletic endeavors and truly enjoys his ties to his community.

The problem as he sees it: He has limited opportunities for advancement and he works for an employer that wants him to keep on doing what he's been doing for several years now. He's committed to staying where he's at geographically, since his ties to his community mean so much to him, but he really does want to keep growing.

Ric keeps asking himself the same question again and again: Should he stay or should he go? If he stays, how can he re-engage or find ways to develop new skills? If he leaves, how and where will he find the type of work he's looking for, especially since he's not sure what he wants to do next (he just wants it to be something different from what he's currently doing)? And, how can he try anything new, given his geographic restrictions?

Meet Joanne

Her challenge? She's in her 30s and she wants to move up and get promoted. Joanne is one of those individuals who seems to energize everyone around her. Family and friends report that Joanne has always had this effect on others; she has always been able to motivate and inspire with just the right words at just the right time.

Joanne knew from her senior year in high school onward that there were two things she loved: She loved learning and she loved leading and motivating others. Her high school and college extracurricular activities demonstrated this: president of her school class; head of her debate team; participation in AP classes in high school; the pursuit of a double major in college; and being active in church outreach activities. Everything Joanne has done, she has done with enthusiasm—and she has always made a positive impact on those she has come in contact with.

Graduating with majors in both education and training and development, Joanne successfully landed a job as a trainer in a growing pharmaceutical company, where she was able to shine as a trainer. And within three years, after successfully completing a certificate program in e-learning, she also received accolades for her work as part of a team that developed several online learning programs to assist employees in the company's remote locations.

Joanne has never stepped back from taking on additional work, including mentoring new employees, helping to strategize custom learning initiatives, or coaching low-performing employees. Through all her work, she has been passionate in her belief in the power of learning to help individuals and her company grow and succeed.

She is equally passionate about helping others to succeed—especially young women interested in pursuing careers in training and organizational development. Because of this passion, for the past two years, she has chaired a regional committee, aimed at reaching out to young Asian-American women and helping them succeed in their first year in college. This same passion fueled Joanne's desire to get her MBA, which she accomplished, excelling as she did in her earlier studies.

While Joanne has never said "no" to an additional assignment, she's been wondering lately if she is doing all she can on her own behalf. She truly wants to move up further in her organization, be recognized for all her hard work, and have the chance to influence company policy when it comes to the learning and professional development of employees at all levels. Her hard work has already made it possible to move up into midlevel management positions and take on the leadership of some special talent management initiatives, and these promotions and leadership roles have helped her make a difference to some extent.

However, Joanne really believes her organization could do much more—to increase its success and that of its employees—and she wants to be a part of making this happen. She also believes her voice would be heard more if she were in a more senior-level position. Now in her mid-thirties, Joanne is serious about her desire to reach the senior-level position in the learning and development area within her company.

Through her years of networking and participation in her local ASTD chapter, Joanne has come to know more fellow professionals who have stepped into the role of chief learning officer at their companies. And the more she has learned about this role, the more she believes that the CLO role is one she wants to move toward.

Where Joanne seems to be "stuck"—which is rather uncharacteristic of her—is in knowing how to best prepare for and apply for this position in her own company. Her organization does currently have someone in the CLO role, but this person is also performing in another key role in the company, causing the CLO position to be less central in moving the company forward.

Although she has significant experience, degrees in appropriate areas, and a strong work ethic, she knows that won't be enough. Because she's always been a self-starter and has relied on her own abilities to learn something new or succeed in a new assignment, she isn't really sure who—or how—to ask for guidance when it comes to her own career development.

Meet Kevin

His career concern right now? He's 63, nearing retirement, but wants and needs to continue working. If you met Kevin at a party or social gathering, your first impression would probably be that he is an especially warm and caring individual. It's likely you would also notice that Kevin appears tired and a bit worn down. And you'd be right on all counts.

Kevin has spent his entire career in the "helping professions." Originally trained and credentialed as a high school teacher, he spent his first seven years out of college teaching economics and social science courses to high school juniors and seniors. Though teaching felt right to Kevin, the high school population didn't seem to be the population that got Kevin excited about his work.

After those first seven years, he landed a job in a community college for a while, where he found that working with adults was truly satisfying. He also determined that a master's degree in adult learning would give him the credentials and training he could use to make a difference and find more work in the post-secondary arena.

One of the professors he met while getting his master's degree encouraged him to consider opportunities in the corporate sector, since he seemed to excel in engaging adults and he also appeared to have a solid understanding of some of the people-related and economic challenges that organizations face. Through some connections his professor put him in touch with, Kevin did some informational interviewing at different companies and eventually applied to one of the companies for a training position.

Kevin got the job and began his new career as a training specialist in a company of about 400 employees that would eventually grow to more than 4,000. His first five years were a dream come true for him: allowing him to combine his interest in teaching, his love of adult development, and his satisfaction with working in a corporate environment.

Then, in the 1990s, things began to change; his company went through a merger and several positions were eliminated. Several employees got a reduction in hours—including Kevin. The newly merged company limited Kevin's role as a trainer, while they also cut the size of the training budget and the company's focus on learning and development.

Bitter about this change, Kevin looked for opportunities in other organizations and found one as a trainer for the staff of a social service agency. Though Kevin initially felt excitement about his new position, the reduced resources and increased demands took a toll on his performance. At the same time, Kevin's wife became ill and he found himself needing to care for her while managing increasing demands at work.

Soon after Kevin turned 60, his wife died, leaving him exhausted, grieving, and unsure of where to go or what to do next. Kevin did decide to return to his training position at the social services agency—but now, three years later, he realizes he needs to find another job where he can once again feel valued and properly compensated, and where he can have some freedom to contribute in ways that use his strengths and skills.

However, Kevin feels he faces several challenges: his age, his latest performance appraisals that reflect his distraction due to recent personal and family challenges, his failure to keep up with the latest skills in training/learning and technology, and his need for an income at a time when there doesn't seem to be many new job openings.

Above all, Kevin knows that he is capable of doing quality work, and he continues to value the chance to help others through his role as a trainer. He just doesn't know how to go forward from here.

You'll get to know these four professionals more in the second section of this book. And, as you get to read about what they are doing to develop their own career strategies, you can do the same. You might also want to keep these questions handy as you read the next chapters.

- Consider what aspects of these four professionals' situations may be similar to your own. How can the strategies they use be helpful to you?

- Or, think about your own specific career development opportunities and challenges at the present time. What do you need to do to move your career forward? Which exercises might help you do this?

Section II of this book will give you several opportunities to dig deeper into identifying your own career strengths and your own areas for further growth. Doing so is a solid first step toward designing your own strategy for making career moves that will be satisfying and rewarding to you. Here's to your career success!

How to Build and Manage Your Career Path

Introduction

Section I gave you a sense of what the future holds for the T&D field, plus the challenges you may face as you progress along your chosen individual career pathway. Our discussion of the present status of the profession and its outlook stressed the exciting and energizing times that practitioners will encounter in the workplace. We also looked at the various job opportunities that are presently available and will be emerging in the next few years.

With roles and responsibilities modified and transformed, new tools and resources being introduced, and the growing impact of workplace and economic trends, it's more essential than ever to take responsibility for managing your career. You'll need to make decisions regarding its direction, journey, interim stops, and ultimate destination. In the face of hurdles, responsibilities, and immediate needs, you may believe that you have no choice but to make concessions about your ideal work environment or remain in a job-that-pays-the-bills situation. However, you always have choices. Do you feel confident and motivated enough to review and select your best option, or would you rather settle for the status quo? If you want to make changes in your work life, then what actions are needed to move closer to your ideal career pathway?

In section II, we present career management guidelines, procedures, and exercises that enable you to make decisive judgments leading to professional achievements and satisfaction. Taking control of determining how your T&D career changes, grows, and expands is a necessary skill for your survival and realization of being a contributing member of your organization and community. Upon retiring, you should be able to look back and feel you had an impact on people through your direct or indirect contact.

At this point, you probably have questions similar to these, but lack the answers:

- As I begin my career, what are some things I need to consider to project a strong and positive impression?

- I know that "up is not the only way" to progress through an organization, particularly with the collapse of the organizational chart and downsizing. What can I do to continue to advance and remain challenged?

- Having been in the field for more than 20 years, what can I do to remain engaged and passionate about my work rather than be in a rut and feeling left behind?

- As I get closer to retirement, I feel that I want to pass on my organizational knowledge, professional experience, and also continue to use my expertise within my community. What are some good ways to do this?

- What can I do to update my job search and marketing/branding skills, learn about social media, and seek some professional coaching to make a career move or a professional shift?

- What skills and knowledge do I need to acquire to better understand and work with multigenerational team members, supervisors, and clients/customers?

The next six chapters will give you practical information and options that can be integrated, where relevant, to the management of your career. Knowing how to plan and strategize is key to being prepared and in control of your professional life. As you gain experience, make moves and shifts, and progress along your career pathway, you will need to redefine and revise your professional image: who you are as a T&D specialist. Remaining competitive and engaged may require further education or that you consider certification options. Perhaps you may want to expand your network or gain visibility by volunteering with your professional organizations, and need to decide what type of activity will benefit you the most. Whether your next work modification is a career move or professional shift, action should be based on information, options, and resources that best meet your goals, and allow you to proceed efficiently and effectively.

You are responsible for your professional life as well as your personal one, and sometimes the two are at cross-purposes. However, with determination, you can integrate and bring harmony to your life, resulting in a well-balanced whole. In this section of the book, you'll be introduced to some basic elements of good career management and provided with the tools, know-how, and latest practices to make realistic and workable plans. These six chapters furnish you with a foundation to design a strategy, including guidelines, procedures, and exercises allowing you to achieve your career objectives.

How to Build and Manage Your Career Path

Once you have finished your reading and completed the exercises, you will be able to:

- Take control of your career management activities for a fulfilling and engaged work life.
- Be more aware of your T&D options and what is best for you and your needs.
- Design a career pathway to achieve your particular goals.
- Understand your professional skills and identify what needs improvement or needs to be learned for progression.
- Prepare for a job search or marketing campaign.
- Imagine more clearly what professional survival and success means to you.

The information you read in section I may have seemed overwhelming and started you thinking about what items are really relevant to you, and how to sort and assimilate this input in a way that is useful to you both personally and professionally. The information that's in the following chapters will help you to become better acquainted with yourself, establish your professional story, and create your brand. You'll be presented with various opportunities for self-assessment and reflection, to review your personal and professional priorities, and develop a detailed vision of your tailor-made future.

Self-directed and individualized exercises have been designed and are located at the end of each chapter. They provide a structure and process to express your thoughts and ideas about your career and the T&D field. These exercises can be used in various combinations at different turning points in your work life, such as when workplace responsibilities and circumstances change, interests and priorities are modified, unplanned life situations occur, opportunities arise, and your professional horizons expand. The information collected and created in your responses to these exercises will become reference-and-review documents.

The case studies introduced in chapter 4 will be followed throughout section II to provide examples of how various career elements and work characteristics can and should be incorporated into a person's decision-making process. By presenting these cases, we hope you gain a clearer understanding of how you can manage your T&D career, the variety of opportunities available, and the professional moves/shifts that can be taken relevant to your present life stage.

In writing this book, we thought more of it as a reference that you could return to repeatedly for guidance and support. As you read and think about the materials for the first time, you will discover career-planning information and practical assessment activities that are useful to you immediately. Other items you'll want to make a note of for future reference. By absorbing the information included in the following chapters, you'll become more aware of yourself, professionally and personally, and find a balance that works for you. And, above all, learn not to have assumptions about limitations and possibilities. Assume positively that with determination, motivation, support, and planning, possibilities exist. You can make a difference, practice your passion, and earn your living through fulfilling and satisfying work.

—Annabelle Reitman

Chapter 5

Progressing Through a T&D Career

Your work is to discover your work and then with all your heart to give yourself to it.

The Buddha

Where are you in your T&D career? Just starting out, advancing within the field, or not far from retirement? No matter what your status is, you need to be able to transition from one professional niche to another. This is part of the process of remaining engaged and challenged in your work. Throughout your career, life circumstances can affect your work performance, necessitate changes in your work life, and modify your professional goals.

You'll need to retain control of constructing your career pathway and understand how to adapt quickly in order to go successfully from point A to point B. As with other career fields, over your working lifetime, expect to experience at least two major career movements or professional shifts, and several minor ones. Some of the modifications are typical adult experiences (advancement); others result from your professional planning (career mobility), personal experiences (parenthood, divorce), or from external actions by others (reorganization). No matter where you are on the pathway from launching your career to approaching the end, the transition process is an important step in a new beginning.

Lakshmi was the first person you met in chapter 4 who is just beginning her T&D career. She is a big "techie" with an instructional design concentration, passion for creating online programs, and interest and ability in foreign language skills. Since she lacks self-confidence, hasn't targeted specific job categories, and is unsure of how to conduct a job search, Lakshmi will need to do preparations such as: work with a coach, develop a plan of action, and become familiar with the tools and resources of marketing herself.

Change often results in uneasy feelings, even when you initiate the changes or believe they're positive. Movements and shifts alter established professional roles, routines, locations, and responsibilities. Home and personal life can be affected as well. The immediate future is a blank space to be filled in and a need to reset your direction. Appropriate and prompt reaction is called for to produce the change outcomes. Taking responsibility for managing your responses and actions to modifications in your work life, you've taken the first step toward success in your new situation.

Transitions

Change is a fact of life, while transition is a process to undergo and complete a change efficiently and effectively. Just as with other career fields, T&D is affected by several emerging career and workplace trends, as discussed by Hecklinger and Black (2010), including

- You and your "job" are being defined differently—organizations are increasingly seeking individuals who perform specific kinds of work for a specific period of time. Begin thinking of yourself as an entrepreneur who markets specialized talents and expertise for HR projects.

- Develop more adaptive or transferable skills for the workplace—advanced technologies, just-in-time deliverables, leaner profit margins, and the doing-more-with-less reality results in the need for skills such as: teamwork, effective communication, problem solving, and critical thinking to remain a valuable and contributing member of an organization.

- Continuing education and professional development is a lifelong activity—Committing yourself to lifelong learning is essential to remain competitive and marketable. This investment isn't an option, as T&D changes and grows, requiring new and updated knowledge and skills.

- Write your story and define your brand. As you continue down your career pathway and its modifications toward your ultimate T&D goal, your identity will also require updates and additions. Professional shifts and career moves, certifications and degrees, professional volunteering, participation in a mentoring program—all are experiences that affect your professional story and alter your brand.

- Review your options of alternative work patterns. Today, you have more flexibility and choices regarding how and when you work, for example; telecommuting, flex time, and social media resources, allowing you to sustain a better work-life balance status. On one hand, with the collapsing of the organizational chart, fewer opportunities exist for mobility and promotions. However, with the introduction of a career-lattice approach to work progression, you now have another set of options.

Whether the change is big or small, the transition process helps you react in a productive way. This process assists in bringing closure to the old situation, giving you some time and space to reflect, re-energize, and settle into the new situation. It allows you to take control of your feelings, whether positive or negative, and be able to acknowledge the challenges you will be facing. A transition interval enables you to gain a clearer picture of your status, make required decisions, and form a forward-looking mindset and professional image.

Kevin Sheridan, in *Building a Magnetic Culture* (2012), discusses the top 10 engagement drivers affecting your attitudes and feelings about your employer and your work. As you review this listing, think about your priorities and needs:

- recognition: feedback, praise, and awards
- career development: opportunities for advancement, lateral/lattice movements, professional development, continuing education
- supervisory/management leadership abilities: have possibilities to utilize these strengths
- freedom and autonomy: able to connect to organization's strategy and mission, contribute to its success
- job content: flexibility, challenges, utilize skills and knowledge, independence
- management's relationship with employees: understand my strengths and challenges, exchange information, make suggestions
- open and effective communication: direct and regular communication with supervisor
- co-worker satisfaction/cooperation: these people are the "unheralded glue" that make you feel good about working where you are, provide support and chances to relax
- availability of resources to perform job: have the necessary tools, equipment, supplies, training, and space to be as productive as possible
- organizational culture and core/shared values: keeps you grounded with your team, and aligned with the organization's mission.

As stated previously, you initiate many changes due to dissatisfaction, disillusion, or disappointment. One clue to this predicament is your disengagement from work. You'll ask yourself such questions as: Am I really involved with what I am doing? Do I feel fulfilled? Is this job meeting my needs? Am I a clock-watcher and can't wait until I finish for the day?

What drivers do you identify that are important to you but that you don't have? Can you think of other drivers lacking in your work that would increase your engagement? Complete Exercise 5-1 Engagement Survey at the end of this chapter. If you're feeling more and more disengaged from your organization and work, what can you do or initiate to become re-engaged or continue to feel productive? Consider making a change in your T&D work or workplace.

Work Modifications: Career Movements

Career movements are general and common job activities, documenting the expansion, retraction, retreat, and direction of a person's work history. Being aware of and understanding these types of work modifications is key to being in control of:

- managing your professional life

- determining its steps and pathway

- developing a new or revised T&D niche

- selecting specific options and resources for your next move.

Most people go through several work modifications in a lifetime, some of which can be experienced simultaneously, such as a promotion and a transfer, or more than once, such as a new job or reorganization. A record of your work history such as an up-to-date résumé is important for documentation and to review your professional story.

Knowing your possibilities is important when examining career objectives and direction, determining your next steps, and developing an action plan.

Some common career movements in the T&D field include
- working for a new employer
- moving within your present organization
- transferring to a new geographical location
- making professional shifts
- retiring.

Working for a New Employer

The most common work modification is accepting a position with a new employer. Most people will change employers, keeping the same role or with new tasks, five or six times within their work lives. Typical questions asked during this transition interval can include: Do I really know what I am jumping into? Will I lose contact with my former work friends? How quickly and easily will I adjust and become engaged with my new responsibilities and work environment? Will I like and get along with my new manager, team members, and colleagues? More important, how will they react to me? Am I really ready for this change?

In chapter 4, Ric was one of the people you were introduced to, who as a Generation X member feels he needs to still expand his horizon. His employer does not have the same perspective. Ric wants to be challenged, engaged, advancing, and learning new skills. Due to ties to his community and desire to find new employment, decisions need to be made about how to best market himself: this may mean considering other T&D arenas, further professional development or certification, rebundling skill sets, or updating job search tools and resources.

Moving Within Your Present Organization

You need to change your mindset and perspective about how you advance along your T&D path. Most likely, it'll no longer be straight up. One of the most recent trends in organization development, as described in chapter 4, is the reduction of the linear career ladder to the emerging career-lattice movement—a lateral approach to career progression. A career lattice focuses on flexibility, continuous learning and development, and qualifying for a range of positions.

Typical questions asked during this transition interval can include: How will this new position affect my home life? Will I live up to the expectations of my new supervisor? Am I really prepared for this move? How quickly will I adjust and be up and running? When will I feel truly comfortable in my new identity? How will my former colleagues react when they see me?

Two major traditional movements still operate as lateral promotions:

- From a staff member to an administrator or supervisor position: This move prompts major modifications in how you see yourself professionally and how you maintain relationships with colleagues. For example, you can now be supervising team members who are friends, and feel uncomfortable about the altered status; or you may be administrating a project whereby some people don't accept you as their peer. This can be a time of excitement and pride in your achievements being acknowledged—you have crossed over to management. You will need time to become comfortable with your new professional image and role as well as to successfully meet the new challenges. Some specific questions to ask during this type of transition interval can include: What management or supervisory training do I need? What should I do to gain staff acknowledgement, trust, and acceptance of me in this leadership role? How can I quickly and easily adapt to my new responsibilities and place within the operations?

- From a middle management to an executive position: This promotion is probably the culmination of all your hard work, sacrifices, and efforts. If you are becoming an executive at a rather young age (before 40), reflect on this major change and its impact on your image, role, status, and expectations by you and others. In this position, you now have direct input into the organization's talent strategies and policies. How do you feel about this? Whatever your age, this is a critical move which calls for thinking about the promotion's impact on you and how to sustain satisfaction in your future endeavors. Some specific questions to ask yourself during this transition interval can include: What exciting projects are on the horizon for me? In what ways will I leave a legacy to the organization? How can I forge stronger outside bonds for the organization and a closer community within it? What do I have to look forward to in the future? Joanne's professional story focuses on her ambition and passion. Although she feels that she's ready to move up to an executive position as CLO, she isn't sure how to best prepare and apply for this promotion. She wants to remain with her present employer, as it is a growing organization and she is in sync with its culture and values. Joanne needs to give herself permission to be on the other side of the fence—to seek help rather than to give it. Some viable options include: establish a mentoring relationship, look into hiring a career/résumé coach, seek advice from other CLOs in her network, or talk to a company HR specialist. Joanne will need to decide what type of help will work best for her.

Transferring to a New Geographical Location

In this move, you actually experience several modifications: a new physical living environment, a new work environment, new work responsibilities, and possibly a new organization. During this time, you and your family will make some larger-than-normal adjustments. Facing several unknowns and risks, you and your family may experience much stress, anxiety, and apprehension.

Relocating and settling into new surroundings entails much preparation and many activities. Due to the schedules set by the employer, you may not have a sufficient period of time to accomplish your personal and work to-do lists. If you have a family, they may need to remain temporarily to complete a school term, complete job assignments, or until new housing arrangements are made. If single, you may be thinking of adjusting to a new life by yourself, and missing your old friends, extended family left behind, and familiar haunts. Typical questions asked during this transition interval can include: How quickly will I adapt to my new work community? What can I do to meet people with similar interests? When will this new location feel like home? Will my family easily settle into new routines and schedules?

Work Modifications: Professional Shifts

At some point, as people pass from early adulthood (their 20s) to middle adulthood (their 30s and 40s) and have accumulated personal and professional experiences, they'll review their lives and work history. Everyone—to some extent—will assess where they began and where they are now, and will re-evaluate where they want to be in the next 10 to 20 years. As a result, career goals and ideal work situations can change. Due to planned experiences and unplanned life events, people grow and develop beyond their original base of interests and capabilities that existed at the start of their careers, and therefore, may experience professional shifts.

Professional shifts are more specific and narrow in scope than career moves. Such shifts refocus how, when, and where workers apply specialized knowledge and expertise. These are often turning points in their career paths.

Five common professional shifts that many T&D specialists consider are
- becoming an entrepreneur
- joining a consulting firm
- crossing over from one specialization to another
- teaching in a T&D or HRD graduate or certification program
- transferring to an outside independent contractor.

Essentially, you have become disengaged from your work and organization; a feeling of "been there, done that" has developed. You're impatient, dissatisfied, and unhappy with the lack of progress with your present employer. This is the time to take control of your career by developing a strategy to regain a sense of fulfillment, satisfaction, and excitement by assessing past and present work situations and envisioning your desired future. At the same time, you need to consider personal and family obligations and responsibilities, present and future ones. What professional shift will fit best with your circumstances today and beyond?

A key element for success in this work modification is to carefully develop a plan of action for this shift. As you carry out the steps and move closer to making the actual shift, review your present professional story and image. You'll need to revise your basic marketing tools to reflect the new and growing professional interests, work arena, and direction.

Typical questions asked during this transition interval can include: Why do I want to make a professional shift and how clear am I about this change? How much am I willing to risk? What support do I need from family, friends, and colleagues? What and how much preparation do I need to do, such as professional development, business plans, marketing strategy, and networking activities? How has my ideal job and work environment changed? What happens if I fail?

Any one of these professional shifts can be a major change in your life, leading you to once again be passionate, challenged, and engaged in your T&D work. Which one will you choose for your next step?

Becoming an Entrepreneur

Some people believe that they have enough experience and expertise to start a business or a consulting service. They may have established a reputation by having their own blog, creating a LinkedIn profile, being active in local professional chapters, publishing, and doing speaking engagements. The idea of being your own boss is very appealing and stimulating. A basic decision is to start it part-time while continuing to work full-time, or to resign and devote full-time to initiating your entrepreneurship planning and activities.

Joining a Consulting Firm

For people who are not ready or willing to assume all of the risk, or if you need the guarantee of a steady income level, this is a viable option. If you have a specialized knowledge or in-depth expertise, such as IT experience, healthcare, instructional design, coaching, multigenerational concerns, or e-learning technology, then you may find yourself in high demand.

Crossing Over From One Specialization to Another

This shift has three options: changing to or adding a new AOE, changing your work setting within an industry, or changing the industry in which you work. To reposition yourself, it will be necessary to target your résumé in a functional rather than a chronological format. It should focus on your professional story and image for the future by highlighting achievements and successes that illustrate your qualifications for the new direction of your T&D career.

Teaching in a T&D or HRD Graduate or Certification Program

Teaching full- or part-time is an option if you have a doctorate degree, an in-depth specialization, and an interest in research. If you think you would enjoy a professorial lifestyle, then look to join a higher education institution. However, you could also conduct certification courses such as the ones sponsored by ASTD and other professional associations. This is a growing arena for T&D specialists who want to contribute to their colleagues' professional development, give back to the HRD community, and aren't interested in academia. Teaching is one way of using curriculum design and delivery skills in a different work setting.

Becoming an Independent Contractor

Independent contract work is a good option when someone wants to take some time off before making a decision about what to do next, such as return to graduate school or gain some specific experience or skills. Signing on with a temp services agency specializing in short-term T&D assignments is a way to create some breathing space, try out various work environments and practice areas, and build up a résumé while keeping an income flow.

Retirement

Almost everyone brings closure to a work life. However, today, due to economic and financial situations, more people are postponing retiring. Nevertheless, the desire still exists to be productive, engaged, and to contribute to the organization. These workers may reduce their work hours or responsibilities, but they still want to make a difference.

If you are a Boomer (born between 1946 and 1964), but are not ready to leave the workplace yet, think about what you still would like to accomplish as a T&D specialist. Do you want to document your organizational knowledge and experience for those who come after you? Mentor some of the new T&D talent? Give back to the community through an organization-sponsored service program?

Still, an official retirement day will come. It's quite common for people not to give much serious advanced thought to what they will do when they no longer need to report to work five days a week. Typical questions asked during this transition interval can include: What do I do now with the extra time in my life? What's my identity at this stage of my life? What have I always wanted to do or learn? Do I (and spouse) want to move to a retirement community, live closer to family, or live in a warmer location?

Semi-Retirement

One option that is becoming more popular is "semi-retirement" careers. In *Second-Act Careers*, Nancy Collamer states, "We (Boomers) intend to work—but this time around, we want to be able to do so on our own terms, on our own timetable, and in our own way. This time we plan to call the shots" (2013). Whether due to need, desire, or a combination of both, many Boomers are or will be searching for ways to rebundle their skills, knowledge, and interests, designing a new and more relevant work mode and format.

For T&D professionals, this could mean considering one or more of the above listed professional shifts that can fit a part-time schedule, such as independent contract work or teaching. Other shifts can provide flexibility and independence, such as consulting and entrepreneurship. Another possibility is using your T&D background as a volunteer for a nonprofit organization. This is the time to follow your passion.

Kevin, our case study who is nearing retirement but wants to continue work, is a good candidate for semi-retirement. He's presently burned-out, disengaged from his work, dissatisfied with his employer, and yet he needs to continue earning an income. He'd like to continue in the T&D field with training, which is a good option for Kevin as a "second-act" career. Looking for a position either in a consulting firm or temp service agency are good choices. Kevin can also consider returning to teaching in a graduate or certificate program. Whatever his decision, he will need to enroll in some continuing education or professional development courses or workshops to update his skill sets and technology knowledge.

Relationship Between Transition Intervals and Career Paths

A career line illustrates your work history. The path it takes traces the overall direction of your work experiences—the unique steps, pace, and the extent of your work story. Transitions mark the specific and individualized ways and changes that have shaped your T&D career. Careers can follow different paths:

- **Vertical:** The most traditional path moves straight upward, representing advancement, increased responsibility, and authority. However, this advancement pathway is being replaced by a career-lattice option.

- **Career Lattice:** Introduced previously, this path is more dynamic and stable than a linear one. Crisscrossing an organization provides opportunities to move to emerging jobs, try out a new area, or depart from stagnant departments.

- **Horizontal:** A lateral move occurs with a desire for more variety in tasks, increased breadth of experience, or new challenges without a promotion.

- **Cyclical:** This path comprises a succession of spirals made to learn new skills or competencies to eventually move to new employment or make a professional shift. Spirals can go in any direction at one organization or can consist of several assignments received from a professional temp agency. You usually return to home base—either your permanent position or the temp agency—before taking on another assignment.

- **Leveled:** A leveled career line is no longer in movement, has stabilized, or reached a plateau. If job engagement is lacking, you are considered to be in a rut or burned-out, such as Kevin.

With each new, deleted, or expanded activity appearing on a career line, a change occurs, thereby causing a transition interval. Your perspective on HRD/business trends, new T&D developments, and satisfaction with your present job situation as well as your ultimate career goals, all influence specific career moves and professional shifts you make and your attitude toward the ensuing transitional experiences.

Work modifications create a temporary blank space in your future that demands time to establish new perceptions of yourself, revising your self-image. Essentially, a transition interval allows you to reconfigure your identity, roles, relationships, and routines. Sometimes this is a major makeover, and sometimes it's minor alterations.

Focus on how these self-defining reference points need to be reshaped:

- **Changing identities:** How would you describe your present professional self? How much or in what ways will this identity change? How do you think others will see you?

- **Changing roles:** What will you be doing that will be new, or if it is the same, how will it be performed in a different way, or with less or more frequency? How will the career move or professional shift affect involvement—at home, or in social and leisure activities? How do others see you functioning, according to comments or remarks said directly to you?

- **Changing relationships:** In what ways will your connections or associations with people at work and with family and friends change?

- **Changing routines:** In what ways will your present home, personal, and work practices and activities be altered, readjusted, or replaced? Are you flexible and do you welcome change, or do you like things to remain the same?

In other words, what will your story be like now? What existing elements will remain relevant? What new elements need to be integrated?

Characteristics of Successful Transitions

To experience a transition interval effectively and efficiently depends on your internal strengths and adaptive responses to change. These are six key success factors:

- Willingness to take a risk or take the plunge: Think positively about the outcomes, which lessens your anxiety about the uncertainty or gamble involved.

- Openness to facing the unknown, entering uncharted territory, dealing with new situations: Prepare by gathering information, setting goals, and making plans.

- Ability to direct, assess, and manage yourself: Self-confidence and self-esteem are solid, and you're able to make decisions and anticipate changes in identities and roles.

- Acknowledgement and sharing of your feelings about these work modifications: Communicate to your network that you are ready to re-establish control over your career, your future, and that you look forward to what life holds for you.

- Development of a support system with people you can rely on for encouragement, resources, and help: Be willing to ask family, friends, and colleagues to be members of this group during your transition interval.

- Competency to deal with stress, frustration, tension, worries: Use appropriate coping methods to stay focused, remain adaptable, have flexibility, and initiate time management.

Think about how these success factors can apply to your identified career move or professional shift. Typical questions to ask regarding how these characteristics can apply to a specific transition interval can include: How relevant is each success factor to my passage through this transition? How can I assess my skills in managing each one? To proceed to the next steps of my career path, can I bundle these factors into an action strategy for the transition interval?

The next chapter presents a key component of good career management strategy: a professional design plan, incorporating your description of satisfying and engaging work, plus your ideal professional image. This is your lodestar, especially as you initiate and experience work modifications, to keep you on track and focused toward the future.

Chapter Highlights

What have you learned? How can this information be applied to your career goals and professional dreams?

➤ Kevin Sheridan discusses the top 10 engagement drivers; list five of the 10 that are relevant to you. (See his listing on page 91.)

➤ Career moves are general and common job activities; list the five most common ones and identify the one or two career moves you are most likely to make within the next three years.

➤ Usually progressing through an organization has been linear; however, the most recent trend is diagonally, known as _____. Do you think this type of move is a possibility for you? Yes_____   No_____

➤ Professional shifts are more specific and narrow in scope than career moves; list the five professional shifts discussed and identify the one career move you are most likely to make within the next two years. (See career moves discussed on pages 92–94, and professional shifts discussed on pages 95–98.)

➤ People aren't fully retiring, but will continue to work in a status called _____. When the time comes for you to "officially" retire, do you think you will continue to work in some fashion? Yes_____   No_____

➤ List the six characteristics of successful transitions, and check off those skills you possess and those you would need to improve or obtain.

1. _____ ❒

2. _____ ❒

3. _____ ❒

4. _____ ❒

5. _____ ❒

6. _____ ❒

Exercise 5-1: Work Engagement Considerations

Exercise 5-1 is adapted from the *Infoline*, "Talent Engagement Across the Generations." Directions: Review the following list of work engagement considerations to develop a picture of your level of work engagement: Check off those you feel are presently in operation for your organization and job.

1. **Attitudes Toward Employees**
   - ❏ Employees are treated fairly by management.
   - ❏ Promotion and advancement are always consistent.
   - ❏ Job promotions and raises are awarded on merit.
   - ❏ Policies concerning employees are administered objectively.
   - ❏ The organization's culture promotes employee well-being and happiness.
   - ❏ People (no matter what level) are treated fairly and respectfully.

2. **Communication**
   - ❏ Communication is encouraged and supported by the culture.
   - ❏ My manager believes in sharing information.
   - ❏ Senior management communicates often with employees.
   - ❏ Co-workers are willing to share information.

3. **Customer-Service Oriented**
   - ❏ Employees are directly responsible for their quality of work.
   - ❏ The quality of products and services are very important to this organization.
   - ❏ Strict criterion for excellence is established and maintained.
   - ❏ The organization understands its customers' needs.
   - ❏ The organization is strongly focused on providing customer service.
   - ❏ The organization considers customer needs as a top priority.

4. **Feedback**
   - ❏ Meaningful feedback is given with improvement suggestions.
   - ❏ Performance reviews are constructive and encouraging.
   - ❏ Reviews are regularly scheduled and are two-way discussions.
   - ❏ I participate in the goal-setting process, including timelines.
   - ❏ Evaluations are fair and appropriate and allow for self-review.
   - ❏ My manager gives praise and recognition for exceeding goals.
   - ❏ I am recognized and rewarded for outstanding performances.

5. **Income and Benefits**
   - ❏ Earnings are compensative for the position and responsibilities.
   - ❏ Income is competitive with what I would receive elsewhere.
   - ❏ Benefits compare to those offered by other organizations.
   - ❏ I am familiar with the value of my benefits package.
   - ❏ The benefits package provides sufficiently for family needs and my own.

6. **Individual Differences and Diversity**
   - ❏ People who challenge the status quo are valued.
   - ❏ I can disagree with my supervisor and feel comfortable doing it.
   - ❏ I feel free sharing my opinions with my colleagues.
   - ❏ The organization strives to attract, develop, and retain people with diverse backgrounds.
   - ❏ The organization appreciates employees with different ideas and styles.
   - ❏ Co-workers and management listen carefully to my ideas and opinions.

7. **Growth Opportunities**
   - ❏ A variety of options are available for professional growth and development.
   - ❏ In-house training and outside learning activities are accessible.
   - ❏ My manager takes an interest in my professional development and advancement.
   - ❏ Tuition reimbursements are part of the benefits package.
   - ❏ Learning from my mistakes is encouraged.
   - ❏ Work is challenging and interesting.
   - ❏ Work is fulfilling.
   - ❏ High performance is acknowledged and rewarded.
   - ❏ There are opportunities to work with a career or executive coach.
   - ❏ The organization offers a mentoring program.

8. Mission and Goals

❏ My priorities and goals are a good match for the mission and the goals of this organization.

❏ I can see how my efforts directly contribute to the organization's overall growth and success.

❏ I feel my job supports the accomplishment of the organization's mission.

❏ My supervisor provides regular information about the organization's mission and goals.

❏ I understand and agree with the organization's strategic goals.

❏ Doing my job well provides a sense of personal and professional satisfaction.

9. Respect for Employees

❏ My manager always treats me with respect.

❏ My manager sincerely listens to my concerns and problems.

❏ My organization appreciates my achievements.

❏ My manager is fair and equitable in granting my requests.

❏ The organization values my talents and skills.

❏ My co-workers care about me as a person.

10. Respect for Management

❏ I respect the senior leaders of this organization.

❏ I respect my supervisor as a competent professional.

❏ Talent is viewed as an asset by the organization.

❏ Senior managers and executives demonstrate strong leadership skills.

❏ I am very satisfied with my direct manager and her work style.

11. Teamwork

❏ Teamwork is encouraged and practiced in this organization.

❏ A strong feeling exists of teamwork and cooperation in this organization.

12. Work-Life Balance: Stress and Work Pace

- ❏ The organization fosters retaining a work and personal life balance.
- ❏ My manager agrees with a work-life balance belief.
- ❏ I am able to meet my job and family responsibilities.
- ❏ I have choices in my work schedule such as flex time and working from home.
- ❏ Work pace enables me to meet expected and required results.
- ❏ The amount of work I am asked to do is realistic and reasonable.
- ❏ The organization has reasonable expectations of its employees.
- ❏ My job does not create unreasonable amounts of stress in my life.

13. Workplace Resources

- ❏ I have the needed resources to complete tasks efficiently and effectively.
- ❏ The newest technology available allows me to meet work objectives and timelines.
- ❏ The workplace is maintained and has a warm, friendly feel.
- ❏ I have a nice, roomy, physically comfortable workspace.
- ❏ The workplace includes areas to relax, eat, exercise, and socialize.
- ❏ I feel safe in this workplace, even when working overtime.

Other topics and questions may be considered for inclusion.

Reactions to responses:

How do you feel about the results? Were the results what you expected to learn? Did you have any surprising results? If so, describe them. Will you take any actions as a result from what you learned about your work engagement situation? Explain.

_____

_____

_____

_____

Chapter 6

Creating Your Ideal Career Path

We are the choices we make.

Meryl Streep

Today's workplace continues to change and transform itself at a more rapid pace than ever before. As a result, people have become acutely aware that they need to have better and more direct control over their lives. This is especially true if you want to do more than merely survive in your job and instead, feel successful, engaged, and living your passion. Some of the seven trends described in chapter 1 have more of an impact than others and will continue to do so on the T&D arena and individual work opportunities:

- New Work and the New Skills It Will Take To Do It

- Shifting Demographics and Increasing Diversity

- The (r)Evolution of the American Worker

- The Talent Trifecta: Recruiting for Agility, Fostering Engagement, and Retaining Knowledge.

Furthermore, considering the probable length of your work lifetime, your T&D role should challenge you to grow, learn, and expand your professional horizons. It doesn't matter where you are on your work continuum; create a vision focused on your desired future career direction and identify the most practical path to reach it. It is never too late to develop this image. When the time comes to reflect on your work history and its accomplishments, we hope it will be with satisfaction, a sense of fulfillment of your career dreams, and realization of reaching your potential.

Having a vision isn't enough; you must transform it into something tangible by setting goals, objectives, and strategies for actually reaching your ideal T&D work. How do you go about doing this effectively and efficiently? What's your first step—where do you begin?

Characteristics of Engaging Work

Feeling good about your work, its outcome, and the rewards you receive is a central point to life satisfaction. When just starting out in the T&D arena or contemplating a career move or professional shift within the field, you should give thought to what it means for you to be engaged in your work.

Work Engagement Characteristics

Chapter 5 listed the top 10 engagement drivers; however, you need to discover what engaging work means specifically to you. How would you describe it?

Engagement is a feeling that's more powerful than just being satisfied, which is an indication of your mood rather than your performance level. You are truly engrossed in what you're doing and have a sense of fulfillment. When professional passion and engaging work come together, your ideal work situation becomes a reality. Consequently, you care about the good of the organization and about doing your best.

> **Taking part in growing and sustaining work engagement is an element of taking control of your career and managing your professional life as a T&D specialist. The benefits include items such as:**
> - interesting and challenging work content
> - fully utilizing skills and expertise in responsibilities
> - outcomes and results that are beyond expectations as achievements
> - being placed on track for mid- and senior-level or lattice positions for desired advancement/movement
> - developmental growth opportunities made available to increase value to organizations and remain actively occupied
> - compensation and benefits that meet needs and are just rewards for efforts
> - looking forward to coming to work every morning.

Values, priorities, and sources of fulfillment vary at different life stages, generational groups, and individual personal experiences. Workplace activities and time spent carrying them out will fluctuate. What was challenging in one phase of your work life may no longer be at some other time. A smooth transition interval from one career move or professional shift to another depends on the clarity of the statement about how and why your workplace values, priorities, and sources of fulfillment have changed. When these three factors are not in sync while doing your job, then conflict, stress, frustration, and unhappiness result.

It is important to be aware of when and why your work situation is no longer dovetailing with your present or future lifestyle, and when you need to rebalance. For example, if you're planning to make a career change into T&D, be certain you know why dissatisfaction exists with your present profession and position. If intending to change T&D areas or organizations, ask yourself what the reasons are for this action. If home and personal life priorities have changed, how does this affect your present or future work plans? If you have vague discontented feelings about your life in general, do you think looking at your present work status will help to restore a better sense of contentment? Do you feel that there's more to work that's engaging than you're experiencing now?

To answer situation questions like those listed above, you first need to describe what engaging work presently means to you. This serves as a foundation for how you'll revise its criteria in the future and be reflected in any alterations to your professional design plan (PDP).

Ric is a classic example of a person who feels burned out, expressing a "been there, done that" attitude, and feeling no longer motivated by his work. He needs to become re-engaged, feel excited, and challenged by what he is doing. At 43 years old, Ric needs to reassess what engaging work means to him now—including the possibility of developing new skills to be more marketable in his present geographical location.

A statement that envisions engaging work includes your ideal:

- job description
- clientele or customers
- scope of the effects of work
- work environment, culture, and location
- team members and colleagues
- organizational mission and goals alignment with values and priorities
- compensation and benefits.

Exercise 6-1 guides you through preparing a comprehensive description of your ideal work scenario. By completing this activity, your individual definition of engaging work and its characteristics will crystallize.

The Professional Design Plan Defined

The key to managing your work life is to draft the larger career picture and then fill in details of your professional goals and your strategies for achieving them. A professional design plan (PDP) is a blueprint for how, when, and where to turn your dream into reality. And just like an architectural project, you'll revise, modify, reduce, or expand it, reflecting changes in your needs, interests, and circumstances. This is a game plan in progress—adaptable, flexible, and reflective of whatever your situation is at any moment as you move through work and personal life experiences. A PDP can evolve and zigzag with applicable changes in the marketplace, business trends, and unexpected events and opportunities.

To design this road, you must:

- Know your life purpose and align your T&D goals with it.

- Be aware of your strengths and weaknesses.

- Commit your thoughts to paper.

- Set accountability checkpoints.

- Focus on reaching your targets, being mindful of barriers and difficulties.

- Track work modifications and career progress.

- Pay attention to details and organization.

- Demonstrate a strong level of commitment to reach your ideal position.

Producing high-quality work performances are the desired outcomes, but it's easy to fall into a rut when you know the job thoroughly, your supervisor is satisfied with your efforts, your work environment is comfortable, and the organization's culture matches your values. Developing a PDP motivates and reminds you to take responsibility for your career by seeking challenges and doing what you consider meaningful, rather than what is effortless and convenient. A PDP is a strategic procedure with a long-term perspective on your T&D career. As a working document, it keeps your attention on your goals and the everyday tasks you need to prepare, improve, and advance steadily toward your ultimate career vision.

The Importance of the Plan

Envisioning your ideal workday, and brainstorming about possibilities—What if I did this? Can I actually do that?—is quite different from writing out concrete and detailed action steps. In committing a concept to paper, what was once vague and idealistic suddenly becomes a realistic and viable probability. By holding a hard copy of your PDP, it becomes a tangible document that:

- gives you the means to work out and refine a strategy to manage your career path and professional experiences

- allows you to develop a workable, comprehensive, and doable action plan to accomplish your professional goals

- empowers you to create a design reflecting what you want, when you want it, and declaring your intentions to yourself and others

- spotlights what you need to do to eliminate gaps in AOEs, expertise, and transferable skills, for preparation to move to the next work phase

- pinpoints a set of related tasks, permitting you to arrange them in logical order

- charges you to action with a format to turn your ideas and dreams into substance

- provides information needed for branding and marketing purposes

- targets the priority undertakings for placement at the top of your to-do list

- serves as a measurement tool for monitoring progress and assessing needed revisions.

Being able to create a PDP is a career management skill that helps you be a successful professional involved in purposeful and engaging work. Furthermore, keeping your PDP up to date keeps your created career vision in sight, preventing things from falling through the cracks. A PDP acts as a baseline for your professional story that you tell through items such as: your résumé, elevator speech, marketing/job search campaigns, and establishing your brand. This plan is central to managing and controlling your career choices for arriving at your desired destination.

No matter your age, or what stage or level you're at in your career, or how much longer you intend to remain working, a PDP is your guide to having an engaging, meaningful, and rewarding work life. This is true for all our four T&D professional examples that represent different generations, needs, professional stages, and personal situations.

The Elements of a Professional Design Plan

With a PDP you can draft, review, and redraft your overall career path and its details as often as needed so that it reflects accurately your updated career vision. Think of a PDP as a template for laying out your career plans and professional activities. Its elements provide a format and space to think about what you need to do, what you are willing to do, and what you can do to achieve your career dream. The PDP elements are aids for filling in the details and completing the picture.

A PDP comprises seven elements:

- ideal professional life summarized
- long- and short-term goal statements
- professional niche
- practical considerations
- action plan
- interim measurable success milestones
- adjustments and revisions.

Ideal Professional Life

A PDP starts with the career vision that you want to reach and live. First review your fulfilling work responses, as your T&D dream job will be based on these answers. Although these two items overlap in characteristics, defining engaging work is an overall comprehensive perspective, while describing an ideal professional life is quite specific so that it truly communicates

- what you want to do

- why you want to do it

- what tasks and activities you would be doing

- where you would be doing it

- what other people would be involved

- what it would feel like to be doing it

- how your life would be different upon achieving your career dream.

This statement explains how using your skills and abilities will benefit others—individuals, organizations, or the profession—and will benefit yourself and your family. It illustrates why what you do for a living is important to you. When the time comes to review your work achievements, you'll feel that you left your mark, however small, on society.

Developing an ideal professional life picture stimulates you to move forward and energizes you into action. It's both a guiding image and a baseline for establishing your goals, objectives, and activities. It focuses your professional desires more easily, creating your unique place or professional niche in the work world. And remember, as priorities and views of engaging work change and diverge, your vision for the future will need to be revised and edited. Lakshmi, who is about to begin her T&D career, needs to develop a clearer and more focused image of her dream career and job. Her passion regarding technology, particularly online learning and social media, the language abilities she possess, and her love of teaching and training is pulling her in several directions. Creating an ideal professional life description enables her to focus, shape, and relate details to what she will be seeking. Having this image in mind will help build her necessary self-confidence.

Long- and Short-Term Goals

Goal statements transform your ideal professional life vision into functional declarations of being specific, individualized, achievable, practical, outcome-oriented, structured, and measurable. Long-term goals encompass the broader picture of what you'd like to occur in three to five years. They represent realization of your career dream and act as a lodestar motivating you to act. Short-term goals have a more manageable timetable of 12-18 months, keeping you focused and clear about what you need to do to progress toward your ultimate goals and how to prevent you from becoming confused or sidetracked.

Professional Niche

A professional niche is created by bundling specific AOEs, competencies, skills (work content and transferable), knowledge, education, and achievements to project a unique professional image or brand identity. Developing a professional niche statement may be your hardest task. This document serves two purposes:

1. It turns the vision of your ideal professional life and its necessary qualifications into a real work situation. Once more, you need to be as detailed as possible. Particularly when thinking about requirements you lack, any that require updating, or any that require expansion. Taking care of these deficiencies become part of your short-term goals and are incorporated into developing your plan of action.

2. It serves as your summary marketing piece for job searches, networking, and promoting yourself within your organization. This statement needs to be concise, succinct, focused, and clear to showcase your qualifications in a powerful and direct way.

Practical Considerations

Professional goals can't be viewed in isolation. Look at them in the context of your overall life goals and current personal situation. This is important not only for maintaining balance between your work and personal life, but also for having the best chance for obtaining the career and professional success you desire. Practical matters need to be taken into account, such as resources and limitations that can act as barriers to moving toward your ultimate work goals in a timely, productive fashion. Kevin, our semi-retired example, wants and needs to continue working, but not with his present employer. Practical considerations are an essential factor in making a decision regarding a professional shift: his age, lack of up-to-date skills, recent poor performance appraisals, and his mindset since his wife passed away. He needs to come to terms with them and also with what actions he will or can take to resolve these considerations.

If practical considerations are not taken into account when setting professional goals, you may face delays, setbacks, and failure with stress and frustration following at home and work. Practical considerations consist of two factors:

- Needed resources: support people, available funds, physical space, equipment, networking groups, and such are the items required to achieve your goals.

- Realistic limitations: family responsibilities, financial obligations, long work hours, travel requirements, health issues, and such are aspects of your life that can restrict amount of time, energy, and provisions available to achieve your goals. To overcome barriers, you'll need to make appropriate and doable adjustments and accommodations.

Action Plan

Career management creates a mindset in which you stop, reflect, and decide on the best course of action for reaching a set of goals within certain limitations. After identifying the realistic issues that influence your career goals, the next step is to create an action plan. The action plan is the heart of a PDP. This is the "How do I get there?" part—the one that initiates your PDP. The majority of your time and energy will be spent carrying out the stages and activities outlined in this document. Strategize carefully and thoughtfully so you will be satisfied and motivated with the results.

Think of each short-term goal as a project needing to be coordinated and completed. What are your procedures and tasks? What are your limitations, resources, and deadlines? Lay out the stages and activities logically, chronologically, and practically with timelines to track progress. The stated stages and activities are your objectives.

An action plan keeps you focused on your destination and its route, preventing you from wandering too far off course. For instance, Joanne knows where she wants to go in her present organization (become the CLO); believes she has the qualifications; and feels that she can make a difference to the employees and her organization. However, she's in a dilemma about how to achieve this goal. Developing an action plan would help her identify (and arrange in logical order), the steps and actions she needs to take for this promotion to happen.

When you have completed all the short-term goals listed for a 12-18 month period, it is time to initiate the next group of stages and activities toward realizing your long-term goal. A PDP of action is dynamic and flexible, allowing you to update as needed. Its directives and tasks should always be within your comfort zone.

Interim Benchmarks of Progress and Success

No matter how carefully you have thought through all aspects of your action plan, if measurable success benchmarks are missing, it's possible not to reach your final destination. Regular checkpoints need to be set up to monitor progress toward a short-term goal. It's critical that you don't head too far along a particular path without determining what's working and what's not. Establish specific calendar dates for a check-off review of completed tasks and activities, or to learn if adjustments and revisions are needed for uncompleted items. Interim benchmarks are important for assessing if your strategies are realistic. This is the opportunity to confirm that your invested time and energy (probably money also) are producing the intended outcomes or whether your PDP needs an overhaul.

Adjustments and Revisions

After you have conducted an interim benchmark review, look at the results. How satisfied are you with the status of your action plan? What items have not been checked off? Give reasons why you did not finish them. Decide what you can do to improve your efficiency and success levels before the next scheduled checkpoint date. Can you reset dates for all or any of the missed tasks? Do any of your short-term goals or their stages and activities require a second look regarding adjustments or revisions? Look ahead to the next few months and note what needs to be completed. Determine if the incomplete items at this checkpoint will have a possible domino effect and make changes as needed.

At times it would be a good idea to refer to your PDP and benchmarked interim results for guidance and information; for example, as part of a yearly life management assessment, for a job search campaign, to initiate a marketing project, or when interested in volunteering for a professional organization.

Turn now to Exercise 6-2. Complete as much as you can at this time. Remember that this is a work in progress, and for some items you may need more time to reflect.

As you put your PDP into action and begin to undergo career moves and professional shifts, you'll experience the ups and downs of transitioning. Moving from one work situation to another—whether it's taking a new position or accepting more responsibilities—will require a change in thinking about your place in the profession. It's important for you to experience a successful and easy transition interval and to be positive about the change in your status. The next chapter will discuss professional development and its role in building and moving your career closer to your ideal T&D professional life.

Chapter Highlights

What have you learned? How can this information be applied to your career goals and professional dreams?

➤ What are the seven benefits of being engaged in your work? List them and check off the ones that are priorities for you.

➤ What are the two purposes of a professional niche? How does this information help you to create your professional niche statement?

➤ What are the seven elements of a PDP? Do you have all the info you need to develop your PDP? Yes_____   No_____

➤ What are the differences between short- and long-term goals? Can you state your short- and long-term goals? Yes_____   No_____

➤ What are the two practical considerations? Do you know what specifically you need to consider as you develop your PDP?
Yes_____   No_____

Exercise 6-1: Defining Fulfilling Work

Directions: Describe what fulfilling work means to you in terms of ideal work goals you would like to reach. This is your dream job—the one to strive toward. This, for you, is the ultimate engaging work. Be as specific as possible about position, workplace, work scope, income, and benefits.

1. What would you like to be doing? Describe your ideal position, including AOEs, competencies, and skills you'd use; roles and responsibilities you'd

have; and activities in which you would be involved. Include if you would be internal or external to an organization.

2. Who would you serve? Describe your ideal audience: employees, clients, or customers with whom you'd be working as well as type of organization and industry or field.

3. Where would you like to work? Describe your ideal workplace. Include work environment, setting, organizational culture and mission, geographic location, and organizational size.

4. What would be your ideal scope of work? Describe how narrow or wide the impact or results of your work would be. Include whether you would work with individuals, groups, or organizations locally, regionally, nationally, and globally.

5. What characteristics would your manager and team members have? Describe the ideal person you would like to work for and the ideal colleagues to work with, enabling you to perform to your full potential.

6. What would be your compensation and benefits? State your ideal yearly income. Describe your ideal benefits package: bonus (if relevant), vacation, personal, and sick leave, medical and dental coverage, plus other benefits that would meet your needs (for example, day care, life insurance, education tuition).

Exercise 6-2: Developing a Professional Design Plan

Part One: Ideal Job Statement, Goals, Professional Niche, and Practical Considerations

Directions: Review your responses to Exercise 6-1: Fulfilling Work and then develop your dream job idea as an ideal professional life scenario—before describing the elements that follow.

1. *Ideal Job Statement:* Write a short summary scenario so that your ideal dream job is up front to inspire you.

   _____

2. *Goal Statements:* Describe your professional goals in terms that are specific and measurable, including a date for completion and the expected results. Explain how they fit into your life goals.

   _____

   • Long-term goals (three to five years):

   _____

   • Short-term goals (one to two years): List as many as you need to prepare to initiate your long-term goals.

   _____

3. *Professional Niche:* Describe the professional AOEs, competencies, skills, knowledge, experience, and accomplishments you plan to bundle to create your customized place in the T&D field. Include both technical and transferable qualifications relevant to the long-term goals listed above. Also include qualifications that you currently lack but plan to obtain and have indicated under short-term goals.

   _____

4. *Practical Considerations:* List all needed resources that can improve your chances of having fewer delays, setbacks, or failures, and then, list realistic

limitations that can be barriers to accomplishing your goals. Be as specific as possible.

Needed resources   **Realistic limitations**

_____

Part Two: The Action Plan

Directions: Think of each short-term goal as a project you need to manage and complete. For every goal statement you listed in part 1 of this exercise, lay out in chronological order the requisite steps or activities, including deadline dates. List as many short-term goals as needed. Take into account the practical considerations that you included above, as you start this listing.

Short-term goal statements _____

Steps and activities to take _____

Deadline dates _____

Part Three: Interim Benchmarks of Short-Term Goal Success

Directions: Set a benchmarking accountability schedule to monitor your progress toward every short-term goal listed in part 1 of this exercise. List as many goals with steps and activities as needed. Set your frequency between monthly and quarterly for best results.

NOTE: Complete this part each time you review the status of your action plan.

Goal review checkpoint

_____

Checkpoint (month & date)

_____

On deadline: Yes   No

Part Four: Plan Adjustments and Revisions

Directions: Review input from part 3 of this exercise and record your thoughts about progress made in completing short-term goals and moving forward toward your long-term goals. Assess what adjustments and revisions are necessary to keep your PDP on track.

NOTE: Complete this part each time you conduct a benchmarking review of your progress.

1. Are you satisfied with the status/progress of your action plan? Why or why not?

   _____

2. What specifically can you do in terms of practical considerations to improve your efficiency and success levels before the next checkpoint date?

   _____

3. What specifically can you do in terms of discipline and determination to improve your efficiency and success levels before the next checkpoint date?

   _____

4. Do you need to make any adjustments or revisions to your PDP to keep it realistically on target and on time? If not, why do you feel changes aren't needed to the PDP?

   _____

If your answer is yes, describe **all** adjustments or revisions needed. Why are these changes necessary? How will they improve your situation and make it easier for you to accomplish your goals? List all needed PDP adjustments and reasons for the changes.

PDP adjustments

_____

Reasons for change

_____

Reward: After achieving each interim success checkpoint and making any necessary adjustments and revisions to your PDP, reward yourself in a fun way for persevering with your evaluation schedule and your accomplishments. If you have completed a project (for example, a certification program or bid for a major contract was accepted), do something special and share your success with family and friends.

Chapter 7

Building Your Career

As you go through life, consider a variety of ways to continue to learn for career and lifestyle purposes.

Anonymous

Given the 2013 revised ASTD Competency Model and future flows of the T&D field, commitment to this profession means that continual development is no longer optional—it's necessary for survival in your future success. Positioning yourself for advancement, changing jobs, emphasizing different skill sets, or expanding your AOEs requires performance excellence. And performance excellence relates to your professional expertise and proficiency. The concerns and reasons that exist for providing staff training and development programs are just as relevant to your situation. Think of why employees attend in-house courses or apply for tuition reimbursement programs—the same rationales apply to your own career goals and ambitions.

In previous chapters we noted that as the field expands, reinvents itself, and integrates many high-technology innovations, that to remain competitive and marketable, you are unable to rely on current skills and knowledge levels—they become outdated fast. Keeping up with new tools, resources, practices, and professional trends is practically impossible without ongoing learning activities. You'll be asked to solve complex human resource problems requiring interdisciplinary approaches and multilevel strategies. Many T&D professionals will find that whether advancing either by the traditional ladder or the new lattice approach, this scenario is the norm.

With changes in the context of practice have come corresponding changes in the nature of roles and functions. Meeting today's, and definitely tomorrow's, workplace demands successfully, you need to regularly review what you have written in your PDP, particularly if your skills, competencies, and knowledge base need updating or expanding. To obtain the learning you need, turn to your own employee manual of staff development offerings and select learning formats in delivery methods to match your specific needs, and work and personal schedules, as well as for practically meeting your objectives. Given today's varied array of e-leaning choices, it's easier than ever to achieve desired growth and development through nontraditional learning.

Commitment to Lifelong Learning

Learning contributes to your overall well-being and mental health, thereby contributing to an extended productive work life that is desired by many more people.

Continued professional growth is a lifelong learning activity enabling you to:

- keep your mind vital and active
- be introduced to new and interesting people and creative ideas
- seek opportunities for challenges
- develop a sense of accomplishment
- broaden your perspective on life and society
- retain a sense of purpose in your life, both personally and professionally
- remain involved and active with family, community, and society at large.

Learning is an ongoing activity through your life into retirement, especially if you want to initiate a "second career." It's never too early to view lifelong learning as a way of living an involved lifestyle, particularly in today's world with people living and working longer, being more active, and experiencing healthier outlooks. Professional development is one way to initiate a lifelong learning habit.

Having professional development activities integrated in your work life isn't only a good career management practice for keeping you engaged, but they also contribute to your success.

Professional development benefits include

- keeping problem-solving skills sharpened, which enables solutions that reflect the most current thinking about specific issues or concerns
- encouraging "out of the box" thinking
- helping to avoid being burned out and disengaged from your work.

- giving you a competitive edge for opportunities and other options with your present employer or a new organization
- providing the most prevalent trends of the field and sharing knowledge about the latest resources and tools
- expanding career options within the T&D profession
- adding credentials to your résumé.

No matter where you are in your career or what work modifications you're considering, in an age of accelerated change and reorganization, continual professional growth is essential to prevent career plateaus and burnout. Consequently, you maintain control over your career's pathway, both in shape and direction.

Keeping up with the latest technology in T&D is a concern of Kevin's as he faces the challenge of finding a new job in his mid-60s. He needs to do some research for training or educational offerings regarding e-learning and the new mobile devices. Kevin will look for local and reasonable cost options.

Basic Elements of Professional Development

Before choosing a professional development course of action, you should be assessing and deciding about subject matter, education or training structure, site, and delivery method regarding specific reasons and desired outcomes. You'll have to check which educational institutions are available locally and identify the skills needed for a work modification. You can easily and quickly opt to attend a professional event like a chapter meeting or a half-day seminar. Not much time, money, or effort is being invested. However, you should be aware of what you would like your return-on-investment to be. Definitely, give more thought to a long-term professional activity, such as a certificate program or a long-distance advanced training course. In making this level of commitment, you want to have a clear and concrete picture about the results. Will it be worth the investment? How much closer will you be to achieving your ideal professional work?

People often undertake professional development activities not because of special goals, but because they feel
- They must stay current in their fields.
- They are expected to participate in professional growth events.
- They might as well take advantage of an in-house training seminar.
- They are the only people not aware of a new tool or resource.
- They should make use of an employer's tuition reimbursement benefit.

It's not uncommon for individuals to try to prepare themselves for a specific role or practice because it's the up-and-coming job to have; it's potentially financially rewarding; or it's a great opportunity that has become available. Obtaining additional learning experience for these reasons can lead to frustration, stress, wasted financial resources, and possible abandonment of earning a degree or certification.

In developing your professional growth goal statements and researching your learning options, you may discover new goals and options that should be considered whether they fit your needs. Determining the most useful learning plan and approach requires some free quiet time and a positive realistic mindset. Then you can create this plan and commit to it. Be reminded that your professional growth needs change throughout your work life; therefore, what was appropriate for you in the past may not work now or in the future.

Joanne, who has a career goal of moving up to CLO, is stuck in understanding how to best prepare for this position. She needs to do a professional development assessment of the weaknesses in her background for this position as well as her best learning options—within a specific period of time. For example, although she has extensive T&D expertise, she lacks general business and talent management skills.

An education plan consists of basic elements that as a unified whole will meet work needs and accomplish future career goals. The plan does this by identifying a specific learning activity, site, and delivery method. Six elements are reflected in the following questions:

1. Why do you want to learn? What are your reasons for this desire? For example, you want more challenging assignments, or you plan to shift to external consulting.

2. What will you learn? What is the subject matter? For example, you plan to update a competency, expand knowledge base of methodology, or add another tool to your resources.

3. Will learning be formally structured? Will you receive accreditation? For example, learning will confer a degree, a certification, or continuing education credits (CEUs).

4. How will learning be delivered? What method or techniques (s) will be used? For example, you will use online training or traditional classroom lectures.

5. Where will you learn? For example, you will learn on a campus, at home, and outside of a traditional location using a tablet.

6. When will you learn? What is the time frame? For example, you will start in six months and complete in two years, or you will attend a one-day professional development workshop sponsored by your ASTD Chapter in two months.

Answering questions provides part of the input for decisions about a learning plan. You should also take into account career goals and present personal life situations and obligations. Refer to the PDP you completed in Exercise 6-2—specifically the goals, steps, and activities established for yourself. Did you list any professional growth interests, including any tentative plans for further education or training? As mentioned before, professional growth goals should always be included in a regularly scheduled evaluation of present work status and place as well as where you want to be.

Professional Learning Options

Options for continued professional development exist today that were barely available since the book's last edition (2006). Rapid and mushrooming advances in technology exist today, influencing delivery methods and thus, leading to even more choices. At various points in your life, different delivery methods, locations, and subject matter with varied combinations will be better matches for your needs. Good career management is using your PDP as a guide, strategizing the best learning combination for you at any given time.

Professional development locations and the delivery methods can be divided into two main categories: (1) employer-sponsored, on-site training and development activities, and (2) off-site education and training activities.

Employer-Sponsored, On-Site Training and Development Activities

As a T&D specialist, you know the pros and cons of learning on site for the employee. However, you may not have thought of them in considering your own situation and needs. Do you need a review? On-site participation means no one leaves the workplace, it is no cost to the employee, and—since training takes place during regular work hours—there is no extra time commitment. On the other hand, on-site offerings may not meet your learning needs or deadlines. Employee workloads may make it difficult to participate in a particular scheduled course, plus their work travel plans can interfere. Or, a more formal, accredited structured program of study may be required.

As you are aware, learning can take place outside a structured environment. The main advantages to this alternative are its flexibility, ability to learn 24/7, and ability to establish your own pace. Do you ever visit the organization's self-directed learning center to review materials and see if any interest you? Can you submit suggestions to the staff member who orders for the center's resource library?

A listing of on-site training and development options includes items such as:

- training classes conducted by internal trainers/instructors or external consultants

- teleconferencing or e-learning (webinars, videos)

- technology-delivered learning (apps, mobile learning, CD-ROM programs)

- online training delivery.

Off-Site Education and Training Activities

A broad range of options exists for continued professional development outside of the workplace. If you work in an organization with available tuition-reimbursement benefits or your department budget has a line item for outside training and development costs, this can be a viable option for you. You need a clear understanding of the type of courses, learning methods, or certifications your employer will support. If you aren't completely familiar with your benefits package, check with the appropriate human resource staff member.

Benefits of participating in learning outside of the workplace include those such as:

- more flexibility in scheduling courses and seminars
- more topical and more delivery methods offered (real-time and web-based)
- availability of degree and certificate-granting programs
- ability to earn CEUs in various arenas
- individualized programs to meet your professional needs
- opportunities for networking and meeting new colleagues and resource people.

A department's budget line item for staff training can be vague or generally worded and thus open to a liberal interpretation. The department manager may have some latitude for how training monies can be spent. With some creative thinking, avenues for learning can be viable that may not have been previously considered.

These are some off-site learning options:

- educational programs offered through a higher-education institution, professional association, or train-the-trainer companies and vendors, such as:

  > degree-granting programs

  > certificate-granting programs

  > professional continuing education courses

  > one-time training events such as conferences, seminars, workshops, and professional chapter meetings (usually eligible for CEUs)

- self-directed technology-delivered courses such as videos and CD-ROMS

- distance-education courses such as webinars and teleconferencing.

For people who are thinking about a career change to the T&D field, or returning to this arena, they should give time to some special considerations. They would most likely be pursuing some professional learning coursework. Review the various options previously discussed carefully and thoughtfully, as you'll probably be paying tuition yourself or seeking some financial assistance, such as loans or scholarships.

Furthermore, certificate and degree-granting educational programs particularly require a full review due to a long-term commitment requirement (from a minimum of one year for a certificate to three or more years for a doctorate) and high financial costs. Ask yourself the following questions before coming to a decision:

- Referring to your PDP, what are your long-term professional goals?

- In what ways would a certificate or graduate degree further or enhance your T&D career, and would it be worth the time and cost?

- What type of program would include your five top-priority skills or competencies and knowledge bases as part of their curriculum?

- Are the program costs within your budget, or are loans, scholarships, or assistantships available?

- Can you go part time or does the program require full-time attendance?

The E-Learning Trend

In many situations, the e-learning approach may be the best choice for continual professional development. These tools and methods are particularly suited for people with busy schedules, long work hours, or travel assignments, but who are disciplined and motivated. Being able to learn 24/7 at any physical location is convenient and accessible. If you are presently a T&D specialist, you're aware of the rapidly growing profusion of e-learning offerings and types of delivery systems.

If you decide that learning via the Internet really suits your needs and goals, another matter to address is the sponsoring organization's accreditation. If you eventually want to apply e-learning course work toward a certificate, graduate degree, or CEUs, the sponsoring organization must be accredited by one of the six regional educational accrediting agencies, by the Distance Education and Training Council, or by a professional organization.

At one time, graduate programs were only offered on a brick and mortar campus, but today you can find diversified online master and doctoral programs with increasing additional options. Conference proceedings and speakers' presentations were once only offered in reprints or recordings. In fact, as a T&D specialist, you will need to be knowledgeable about e-learning deliverables for your work performance expectations. The excuse, "I'm more comfortable designing curriculum for the classroom or delivering person-to-person" is no longer acceptable. With the expanding use of devices and methods such as tablets, MP3 players, smartphones, apps, notebook computers, and social media modes such as blogs, Twitter, Facebook, LinkedIn, wikis—m-learning is rapidly becoming the major sub-division of e-learning. This is definitely the future as more young adults enter the workplace that have grown up with the Internet and mobile devices as part of the resources used in high school and higher education.

The term *m-learning* as defined by *Wikipedia* is: "Any sort of learning that happens when the learner is not at a fixed, predetermined location, or learning that happens when the learner takes advantage of the learning opportunities offered by mobile technologies" (2013). Its objective is providing learners the flexibility and convenience to acquire needed learning anywhere and at any time. M-learning is also collaborative: People can share instant feedback and tips.

Since Lakshmi is very familiar and comfortable with technology and online learning, she can address her shyness and ability to market herself through researching short courses or workshops offered through a webcast, a video, or an online course about presentation and interview skills.

Personal Lifestyle Factors and Learning Options

Learning activities, for the most part, mean less involvement in other undertakings. Take a look at how your time is spent and what are necessary adjustments to your schedule and activities plus what you can give up to make room for professional development.

Personal and Work Factors

If you decide to pursue further professional education or training, it involves more than just taking into account various learning approaches with their specific features. Another factor must be looked at: your personal, family, and work schedules, responsibilities, commitments, and free time available for learning pursuits. Priorities affect planning for work modifications, particularly those requiring a good amount of your time, effort, or money.

First, let's review your PDP to identify existing personal or family constraints that may require consideration when developing a plan of action for continued professional development.

Consider these questions:

- Do you have children and child-care responsibilities?

- Are you a single parent?

- Are you responsible for aging parents?

- How much time do you devote to family and personal activities?

- What are your volunteer commitments?

- If necessary, do you have sufficient finances to cover the costs for the learning activity?

- If married or in a committed relationship, is this person an advocate of your plans?

- If you would like to pursue a long-term educational commitment and have children living at home who are 12 years or older, how do they feel about you returning to school? Are they aware of the home adjustments that may be required?

Now, let's take a look at your work situation and review these factors:

- average number of daily or weekly work hours, including any overtime
- a reasonable commute between home, workplace, and campus (for real-time learning)
- demands of project or deadline-based work
- amount of travel for work
- amount of and frequency of taking work home.

If you are interested in attending an off-site educational program, but feel that your work lifestyle is not in sync, discuss it with your manager and see if an adjustment can be made in your work schedule. Perhaps you can work flexible hours or work from home a couple of days. Emphasize the benefits that your department and organization will receive by the pursuit of your desired professional development goals.

Turn now to Exercise 7-1 to identify the personal and work lifestyle factors and constraints.

Education and Training Options

After you have compiled information and dates from your PDP, reviewed lifestyle factors and constraints, and researched initial education and training alternatives, it's time to select the best learning or approach for you. Exercise 7-2 enables you to prioritize your learning options and identify preferences in terms of selection criteria. It's possible that your learning strategy ultimately may involve several procedures. For example, you decide to apply for a certificate program and register for both classroom and online courses because of persona or work lifestyle concerns. The end result is the development of an action plan for your continued professional growth. Details of this plan should be incorporated into your PDP, ensuring that it can and will fit into your overall career plans and be a part of your regular self-assessment.

The next chapter adds other dimensions to professional development and growth: volunteerism and mentoring as alternative ways to learn.

Chapter Highlights

What have you learned? How can this information be applied to your career goals and professional dreams?

➤ What are five of the seven benefits gained from being committed to continued professional development? Which ones are most applicable to you?

➤ What are the six benefits of participating in a continued professional education site? Which ones are most applicable to you?

➤ What are the six elements of an educational plan? Do you have all the input you need to make a decision about designing your education plan? Yes____ No____

Exercise 7-1: Assessing Constraints on Your Learning Options
Part One: Lifestyle Factors
Directions: Review the listed personal and work life factors and check off all that are relevant for you. For each one checked, indicate: A) the percentage of time allocated weekly, B) the level of financial resources allocated monthly, and C) the priority you assigned to that factor, from 1 (high) to 5 (low).

Personal lifestyle factor	A) % of time	B) % of budget	C) Factor priority
Working parent			
Single parent			
Care for aging parents			
Basic living expenses			
Recreation/physical fitness			
Family time/activities			
Medical costs			
Commuting/work costs			
Volunteering/community services			
Other			

Work lifestyle factors	A) % of time	C) Factor priority
Length of commute		
Number of work hours		
Travel frequency for work		
Work taken home		
Project/deadline-based work		
Other		

Part Two: Constraints on Your Learning Options

Directions: If any of the factors have been checked in part 1, complete this section for a clearer awareness of the constraints on your selection of a learning strategy. (If none were checked, your selection of a learning strategy will be largely based on your career plans and personal preferences.)

1. Based on your responses in part 1, list a maximum of three constraints that will most likely affect your decisions about continued professional development.

2. In what ways will these constraints influence how you go forward with plans for further education, training, or certification? (For example, a single parent may opt for part-time graduate work on online course delivery.)

_____

3. What personal or professional support is needed to initiate professional development plans successfully or reduce the stress that may arise from adding another activity to my schedule and calendar? (For example, a supervisor's approval is needed to attend seminars or a workshop during work hours, or family's support is needed for taking weekend courses.)

_____

Exercise 7-2: Select Your Best Professional Development Option
Part One: Identifying Learning Objectives
Directions: Considering your career objectives and professional needs, state the AOEs, competencies, skills, and knowledge you would like to learn or update, enabling you to be more qualified and marketable as you progress on your career path. Describe your learning objectives in a two- or three-sentence paragraph:

_____

_____

_____

Part Two: Prioritize Learning Options
Directions: With any input from the lifestyle factors assessment from Exercise 7-1, review the learning structure, delivery methods, and site options listed below. Indicate three options that interest you the most and that are viable for you. Rate their priority on a scale of 1 (high) to 3 (low).

Learning Structure	Time Commitment	Convenient Schedule	Fair Cost	Financial Aid	Program Standing	Career Need
Master's program						
Doctoral program						
Certificate program						
CEUs						
Noncredit seminars or work-shops						

Learning Delivery Methods	Flexible Schedule	Custom-ized Study Course	Inter-active Method	Self-Paced	Affordable Cost	Career Need
Real-time lecture/ presentation						
Webinar/ video						
Skype						
Online courses						
M-learning						
Other						

Career Expansion Via an Alternative Learning Experience

Be a student by staying open and willing to learn from everyone and anyone.

Dr. Dwayne W. Dyer

In addition to educational and training venues, people can look for professional learning opportunities through alternative learning options: volunteer and mentoring programs. They may want to customize their learning experience to meet an individual improvement need. Often, a volunteer assignment or mentoring relationship satisfies other interests, such as gaining specific skill experience or increasing network circles.

Volunteerism and mentorship are two very different activities serving different purposes, however, the element of learning exists in both programs—they are just delivered differently. You need to decide if participating in both, one, or none would be worthwhile. The information provided should help you with this decision.

Identify Goals and Needs for an Alternative Learning Experience

Whether you think you should volunteer or participate in mentoring, you should use the same decision-making process for setting desired learning outcomes. Much can be gained from a non-classroom learning activity if you give careful thought to the why, what, and how of your involvement. Manage your alternative learning experience by taking time to think and be certain about your present professional status and desired future direction. Then review your volunteering and mentoring options and make the best selection for you.

Be as clear as possible about the work modifications you want to make. What AOEs, competencies, skills, or knowledge bases are you lacking? What do you need to update or expand? Which deficiencies can be filled through volunteerism, or which weaknesses can be strengthened by a mentoring relationship? Your answers can facilitate how you identify a specific attainable alternative education opportunity that meets your needs.

Turn to Exercise 8-1 that focuses on the personal rewards and professional development goals of this type of activity. Complete it before exploring alternative learning possibilities.

Volunteerism

Our focus is basically volunteering within a professional organization. For the most part, this refers to chapter activities, committees, and boards. Some people will move from working on the local level to become involved at the national level with its diverse opportunities. People participate in managing a professional chapter to:

- network with colleagues

- increase visibility to market themselves

- gain experience with a specific skill or knowledge set

- demonstrate leadership abilities

- strengthen validity of their résumés

- try out new materials and tools in front of an audience

- share information, opinions, and experiences with associates

- help a professional group conduct business and thereby, give back to the profession.

If your professional organization offers an orientation or retreat for volunteer workers and leaders, it's a good idea to take time for reflection before attending any of these activities. When you have a complete picture of personal and professional volunteer goals, you can select sessions to attend and complete the exercises so that they will be the most beneficial and meaningful.

As part of your volunteering decision-making process, ask for a position description. Many organizations have written information about their major volunteer positions, for example, board members and committee chairs. If this information doesn't exist, then talk with one or more of the following people: a person presently in the position, chapter president, or board member whose portfolio includes the position. Find out what the expectations are for tasks, time commitment, and requisite or preferred skills and experience. Draft an amended job description that meets your learning objectives for submission to the appropriate person(s) for review and discussion. This prevents miscommunication about responsibilities, expectations, and leeway to gain the knowledge, skills, and experience desired.

Typically volunteers identify a particular position or activity based on available assignments, interest, time they can commit, and the requisite qualifications. They seldom think about how this experience may enhance their professional development and that they may be able to shape the assignment for their learning needs. To give the matter adequate consideration, you can develop a job description, set objectives and activities, and define outcomes for a volunteer position just as you would for a workplace position.

You may want to consider other volunteer avenues beyond professional organizations. One possibility is the communication arena: writing articles, making presentations, and facilitating workshops/seminars. Your workplace is another possibility for volunteer opportunities. Community service projects may be sponsored by the organization and need people to plan staff or client events. A local community service agency or program may welcome your professional background by having you involved in activities such as serving on its board, conducting work skills workshops, or developing training guides. These types of experiences can have learning outcomes and can provide some of the benefits described below.

Volunteering Benefits

Given the hectic work and personal lives that most people live, it's a more effective and efficient use of time to gain more than one benefit from an activity. Why not view volunteerism as an experience-based approach, whereby work on an actual project or real problem can accomplish some specific learning objectives of your own? For example, serve on a membership committee to increase your marketing skills or on a board to strengthen leadership abilities and acquire needed experience. Establishing tangible learning objectives will further your engagement in volunteerism and its challenges.

> **Before exploring volunteer options or deciding to accept when presented with an opportunity, ask yourself some questions such as:**
> - How can a volunteer position help my career and move me a step closer to my professional goal?
> - In addition to experience, what other outcomes do I want from volunteering?
> - What expectations do I have of this particular assignment?
> - Do I know the expectations the chapter board or on-site staff has of me?
> - What success benchmarks do I want to establish?
> - How much time and energy can I realistically give to volunteerism?

Consider a professional organization as a learning environment and therefore, you can adapt some of your T&D principles and applications to the volunteer position—for example, design a needs assessment, or videotape a program. Perhaps you can offer to manage the chapter's job bank. Refocus your perspective of high-performance work and learning toward your volunteer experience.

> **Volunteerism and workplace learning share some of the same characteristics:**
> - A need exists to create, extend, and apply knowledge for high performance.
> - The focus of learning models is on the learner rather than the trainer.
> - Learning is an active process that involves the individual taking responsibility for what is learned and how the learning occurs.
> - Experience-based learning—acquiring skills and knowledge by doing—is one of the best educational methods for some people.
> - Learning activities stress performance improvement and expansion of a person's knowledge base.

Volunteer Activities Support Career Goals and Needs

In viewing volunteerism from a learning vantage, you and the professional organization can profit. Think of this activity as part of your career management responsibilities and include it in your PDP. If you are transitioning into the field or a different area of the profession, this can be very beneficial.

Remember when you did an internship or a field service project as part of your graduate or undergraduate studies? Those experiences were usually linked to your major or professional specialty, with education and training objectives developed and integrated into the experience. Before beginning your position, you prepared and researched relating to the outcomes desired. Once more, take a similar outcomes-focused approach by reviewing your PDP for your responses to the questions listed on the following page.

- Professional goals: Where do you want to be one year or three years from now? Even five years?

- Career mobility: What kind of career moves or professional shifts do you need to make to achieve your goals?

- Personal needs: What personal objectives and constraints should you take into account?

- Professional needs: What competencies, experience, or knowledge do you need to gain or update to be ready and qualified for your work modifications?

- Self-directed learning: Which of your professional development needs can be met through non-classroom activities?

- Volunteer assignment: How can you gain some requisite learning experience to increase your marketability and competitiveness?

It's important to know how to leverage volunteering with the organization or how to align the group's goals and needs with your skills, available time, and interests. Set reasonable expectations for yourself so that at the end of the assignment you feel you've accomplished something worthwhile and made a contribution. You take control of your volunteer work by deciding what you want to learn or experience, how you intend to accomplish it, and how benchmarking will take place.

Lakshmi, if not already a member of her local ASTD Chapter, should join and become involved in its activities. With her technology savvy and online learning and social media expertise, she can become a valuable and desired volunteer chapter contributor. This is a good way to gain self-confidence, add some experience to her résumé, and learn about job openings through networking and the chapter's job board. An added benefit is that Lakshmi may have opportunities to meet and become known by some T&D hiring authorities.

Ric could also benefit from volunteering in his local ASTD Chapter. He already believes in community service with his work with local student populations and his children's athletic activities. Volunteering for his local chapter would give him an arena to gain new skills, meet good resources for informational interviews, and acquire new contacts for job leads.

Develop a Learning Agreement

Writing out your goals and objectives as a tangible document helps you commit to your learning needs. A volunteer work-learning agreement outlines your intended learning targets while accomplishing your assignment. This effective tool allows a better match between your learning and performance objectives and the tasks of your position. The contract is a self-directed agreement that is explicit and concrete, spelling out document details. Elements of a volunteer work-learning agreement are

- summary statement of the general project or activity: mission, purpose

- job description: boundaries, conditions, time commitment, and outcomes

- position or role objectives: learning goals reflected in AOEs, competencies, skills, and knowledge to be acquired

- activities of the position: role (title), tasks, responsibilities, and identification of where and how learning will occur

- evaluation and performance methods: benchmarks for self-review

- your signature: affirmation of your commitment

- a witness's signature (optional): can be a professional colleague, mentor, or coach.

A written volunteer experience agreement has the following advantages:
- helps to spotlight exactly what will be accomplished and how it will be done
- provides tangible evidence of your intent
- enables you to stay on target
- prevents others from misunderstanding your responsibilities
- allows for scheduling intermediate progress checks.

Turn now to Exercise 8-2 and develop your own volunteer work-learning agreement.

Evaluate the Volunteer Experience

If your organization doesn't have a formal means for review of volunteer experiences and how people are doing, establish an evaluation tool yourself. After about two months and again during the second part of the assignment, informally review your progress toward accomplishing your learning objectives and meeting expectations by responding to these questions:

- How do you feel about your progress in completing this assignment?

- Do you still want to acquire this learning? If not, why?

- Is there a new learning objective you'd like to add? What is it?

- Does the volunteer work-learning agreement need to be amended to reflect changes in your thinking? If so, what are the changes?

- If changes are desired, can the agreement be revised? To alter the actual assignment, does someone else need to be involved?

As with any work situation, evaluating your performance and looking at benchmark successes are important. Similar to a paid job, an assessment of accomplishment level and quality is done from two perspectives: the organization and the individual. Most likely your association provides feedback when an assignment ends, assessing the extent to which volunteer performance met the group's objectives and success criteria. These procedures probably focus more on the project or team's benchmarks than on your goals.

However, it's important to conduct your own evaluation that stresses how sufficiently learning objectives were fulfilled and the level of your personal satisfaction with the experience. This assessment should target three areas:

- level of satisfaction and overall rewards received

- extent to which the experience met your personal and professional needs

- documentation or evidence indicating learning has taken place.

This review is a learning experience in itself. Did you have unrealistic expectations about the assignment or the role that volunteerism can play in your professional development? The outcomes can be the basis for seeking and accepting future volunteer work and for structuring the position to accommodate specific personal and professional interests and desires.

Exercise 8-3 can complement any final evaluation that your association may make available or it can substitute for a formal review. Before beginning this final evaluation, gather together your learning agreement and any informal review information you may possess for accuracy and thoroughness. If you have used a coach, mentor, or colleague as a sounding board while involved in the assignment, discuss the assessment outcomes with this person. It's a good way to gain closure and celebrate with someone who has provided support during the experience.

Remember to save copies of all relevant materials—reports, brochures, photos, videos, blog comments, PR pieces, finished products, any original work, and presentation evaluations—to document learning and accomplishments resulting from the activity. These items can be part of a portfolio of your strengths and expertise. They are also the basis for the addition of skills, knowledge, and achievements when updating your résumé, developing your professional story, and creating a brand for marketing purposes. This information regarding your alternative way of acquiring T&D knowledge and experience helps establish the credibility needed for advancement, job changes, or moves from an internal position to your own business or practice.

Mentoring Program Participation

Involvement in a mentoring program can be very rewarding and satisfying, personally and professionally. Lois Zachary believes, "The purpose, the process, and the product of a mentoring relationship is learning" (2009). This is an opportunity to learn on a one-to-one basis with a person who has the expertise and experience you seek and who is willing to share their knowledge with others. The ideal outcome is a two-way interaction exchanging insights, information, competencies, and experiences in organizational, personal, and professional arenas. These relationships are often long-term connections that are sustained after the formal association has ended. The following discussions about mentoring are based on work developed by Annabelle Reitman and Sylvia Benatti. For more information, look out for their upcoming book in 2014.

Mentoring Process Characteristics

Mentoring programs can vary from organization to organization in format, style, and operations. Regardless of the model or design, they all have comparable goals and objectives to help participants grow and develop so as to perform at a higher performance level and sustain work engagement.

The basic components of the mentoring process include

- developing skills and competencies for fulfilling career goals and professional proficiency
- examining future career direction and possible moves and shifts
- acting as a sounding board to actively listen and ask the questions that lead people to look at their situation realistically and practically
- sharing life experiences, specifically those dealing with risks, difficult circumstances, or unknown elements
- giving support and encouragement to seek new challenges, not become discouraged, and to preserve knowledge.

Whether you are a senior executive or are beginning your T&D career, you can benefit from participating in a mentoring program. Increasingly, a mentoring relationship is collaborative rather than a person who is an authority figure (mentor) and a young person who receives the wisdom (mentee). Learning goes in both directions in give-and-take discussions and activities that both participants agree upon. For example, a Boomer generation executive may want to acquire more technology savvy skills, while a Generation Y person may want to become more aware of the organization's culture.

Mentoring Relationship Characteristics

> **For learning to take place effectively and successfully, a mentoring relationship needs to include**
>
> - being aware of and acknowledging each other's needs
> - establishing and sustaining trust, openness, and authenticity in communication
> - committing to the relationship
> - defining learning goals and objectives
> - setting timelines
> - respecting each other's work and communication styles
> - conducting scheduled reviews of education progress
> - building a productive and strong work collaboration.

As you can see, involvement in mentoring requires serious thought about the time, effort, and willingness to do your part in having a rewarding and satisfying relationship. Develop a clear picture of the person you would want to match with and the resulting learning outcomes.

NOTE: A mentoring relationship is usually long-term—from a minimum of six months to two years to beyond. It ends when the two individuals feel that no more can be gained from continuing to meet. However, they remain in contact, are part of each other's network, and when needed, act as sounding boards or advisors.

Mentoring Supports Career Goals and Needs

Mentoring programs can be found in one of two ways: Your organization may have established one as an employee career development service, or the local chapter of a professional association may support one for its members. Similarities exist between volunteerism and mentoring regarding achieving your career goals—so consider mentoring in the same light as volunteering, as part of your career management responsibilities, included in your PDP, and as quite beneficial when transitioning into the field or a different area of the profession. This is another appropriate time for an outcomes-focused approach and a review of your PDP for information related to how mentoring can help you:

- achieve your short- and long-term goals
- make a necessary career move or professional shift
- acquire necessary competencies, experience, or knowledge to be ready for a desired work modification
- conduct some self-learning non-classroom activities

- gain some requisite experience to increase your marketability and competitiveness.

The information you gather provides the basis for your decisions about what you want to learn or experience, how to shape a meaningful relationship, and how benchmarking occurs.

Looking at Joanne's situation, it would seem that she could benefit from participating in a mentoring program, either within her organization or local ASTD chapter. Being involved in a mentoring relationship at her workplace would give her the advantage of meeting with someone familiar with the organizational culture and politics. Since she knows numerous CLO professionals from being active in her ASTD chapter, she could ask one of them to form a mentoring association to help her in preparing for this role.

People involved in a mentoring relationship bring a positive mindset to:

- Spend meaningful time in focused two-way sessions.
- Create an environment that encourages being open and honest about feelings, concerns, perspectives, and responses.
- Share knowledge and thoughts about the organization, its culture, and values.
- Allow reactions to frustration and anxiety to be expressed, providing candid and constructive feedback.
- Reinforce "lessons learned' when a washout happens and reinforce that risk-taking is OK.
- Foster expanding horizons, trying out new roles, and practicing newly learned skills.

Mentoring Agreement

Establishing a written agreement prevents miscommunication and misunderstandings. A signed document sets up the ground rules for organizing the sessions, identifying learning goals, defining boundaries, creating a work plan with strategies, and describing accountability procedures. This constructs realistic base lines to mentoring activities and their outcomes.

If your mentorship is part of an organization's or a professional association's sponsored program, then most likely an evaluation form, instructions, and process exists. Otherwise, you and your partner need to set up your own using the agreement form in Exercise 8-2 as your guide. Participants should be able to set up and carry out this formal arrangement for the mutual benefit of both parties. The elements of this agreement consist of:

- clear and focused, stated goals

- work plan outlined for learning activities and resources used

- success criteria and assessment means

- ground rules for a productive and harmonious relationship

- set boundaries and barriers to prevent misunderstandings

- procedures for resolving stumbling blocks

- review of mentoring relationship status and progress toward goals.

The agreement form is signed and dated by both parties. Upon completion of stated goals, if they would like to continue the mentoring relationship, then the agreement needs to be revised.

When differences exist regarding such matters as opinions, procedures, and roles, individuals should act as professionals with respect for each other, and be able to compromise to the satisfaction of both.

Evaluate Mentoring Progress and Quality

Learning doesn't happen without ongoing feedback: Are we both on the same page? Is there give and take in our relationship? Do we both feel we are benefiting from this association? A strategy for evaluating mentoring outcomes for both individuals and the established timelines is the key to a successful mentoring relationship. This includes holding interval assessments as well as a final one. Similar to volunteerism, a review of the relationship's quality and the progress toward goals is a form of learning. After both mentoring participants complete a written evaluation, they come together to discuss their responses and mutually decide how the mentoring process and their meetings can be improved.

As with the mentoring agreement, your organization or professional association may have an evaluation tool in place. If not, then set up your own such as in Exercise 8-3, an accountability checklist—a base guideline for achieving milestones and making adjustments to the mentoring agreement.

This mentoring assessment should target five areas:
- level of satisfaction with experience and overall benefits gained
- extent to which relationship met personal and professional needs
- documentation or evidence indicating learning has taken place
- frequency of timelines achieved, both short- and long-term
- effectiveness of meeting sessions.

Accountability is essential for developing and sustaining a meaningful and fulfilling relationship. A successful mentoring experience involves mutual trust and respect, plus a high level of professional behavior and civil communication. Authenticity exists throughout, and at all levels, that is reflected in the evaluation.

We're about to tackle the final phase of realizing your chosen career move or professional shift: marketing yourself. In the next chapter you'll learn the importance of knowing your professional story and developing a marketing strategy for promoting your T&D strengths for job search, advancement, and business development purposes.

Chapter Highlights

What have you learned? How can this information be applied to your career goals and professional dreams?

➤ List a minimum of five of the eight reasons people volunteer in a professional organization. Check off those that are applicable to you. If none, why?

➤ What are the five characteristics that volunteerism and workplace learning share? Would volunteering support your career goals and needs?
Yes_____   No_____   Why?

➤ What are the seven elements of a learning agreement? Do you have sufficient input to develop a learning agreement for volunteering and for having a mentoring relationship?   Yes_____   No_____

➤ Identify the two arenas in which you can find a mentoring program. Which one would work best for you?

➤ What are the basic components of the mentoring process? Would this type of learning activity support your career goals and needs?
Yes_____   No_____   Why?

Exercise 8-1: Identify Your Personal and Professional Needs

Directions: Identify professional needs that can be met through a volunteer and a mentoring experience. Answer the following questions as thoughtfully and fully as you can. Think about your responses as you explore volunteering and mentoring opportunities. If you've already accepted a volunteer assignment or are participating in a mentoring program, complete this exercise as soon as possible to gain the greatest benefit from the experience. If you are participating in both types of alternative learning activities, complete the form for each activity.

Circle whether this is for a *volunteer* or a *mentoring* experience. If already volunteering or in a mentoring relationship, describe its characteristics, the people involved, and current time length.

Personal Needs

1. Explain why you are interested in this type of experience—your personal objectives.

   _____

2. What would give you the most satisfaction from this experience?

   _____

3. What outcomes do you expect from this experience?

   _____

4. Do you anticipate any drawbacks from participating in this experience? If so, what are they? If not, why not?

   _____

5. How much time can you realistically give, or want to give to this program?

   _____

Professional Needs

1. Describe the AOEs, competencies, skills, and knowledge that will be involved in the experience.

Qualifications	Needs to be used	Acquire/Improve/Update
AOE:		
Competency:		
Skill:		
Knowledge:		

2. What other outcome would you like to gain from this experience?

   _____

3. Overall, how can this experience contribute to the progress of your T&D career?

_____

4. How do you plan to achieve your learning objective through this experience? For example: activities, role, tasks.

_____

Exercise 8-2: Checklist for Developing a Learning Agreement

Directions: Before starting a volunteer assignment or beginning a mentoring relationship, review your answers in Exercise 8-1. A written learning agreement ensures accountability. It confirms and avoids misunderstandings about desired learning outcomes and the means for accomplishment. The agreement outlines strategies and work plans for creating and strengthening a successful, satisfying working relationship. Conduct interim reviews of your activities to track your learning progress.

If you are participating in both types of alternative learning activities, complete the form for each activity.

Circle whether this is for a *volunteer* or a *mentoring* experience.

Describe the activity and your role, responsibilities, tasks, timelines, amount of time commitment, and other people involved. Explain how this experience will advance your career or help you accomplish your professional goals.

Use the following checklist to take into consideration items relevant to your learning situation that need to be included in an agreement.

Learning Objectives	Item	Describe	Check-off
Specific learning activities or work plan			
Tools/resources to be used			
Success criteria/measurement			
Communication methods			
Any boundaries/barriers			
Interim learning review			
Final accountability review			
Documentation of learning and achievements for future use			
Signatures and date			
Witness signature (optional)			

NOTE: As this experience progresses and expands, it may become necessary to change or amend one or more of the items included in the learning agreement; particularly after an interim learning review.

Exercise 8-3: Evaluate Your Alternative Learning Experience

Directions: Fill out this evaluation form within two weeks of completing your learning activity, while the experience is still fresh in your mind. Refer to your learning agreement and any interim review information gathered while involved in the activity to help you respond as accurately and completely as soon as possible. Is there someone you can share your responses with to bring closure to the experience and perhaps, celebrate?

If you are participating in both types of alternative learning activities, complete the form for each activity. Circle whether this is for a *volunteer* or a *mentoring* experience.

Describe the activity and your role, responsibilities, tasks, timelines, amount of time commitment, and other people involved. Explain how this experience will be valuable in reaching your ideal job.

Accountability Items

How successful would you rate this learning experience and why?

100%   75%   50%   25%   0%

List your expectations that were met and unmet by this learning experience.

_____

If you indicated that all or some were met, briefly give one illustrative activity for each item listed.

_____

If you indicated that one or more were unmet, explain why that happened.

_____

In what ways did this activity meet your personal needs? (Refer to Exercise 8-1, Personal Needs.)

_____

What AOEs, competencies, skills, and knowledge bases that you identified as important professional needs were you able to integrate into the learning activity? For those qualifications listed below, indicate how they were integrated into the activity.

Qualifications Used	Acquired/Updated	Improved/Omitted
AOE:		
Competency:		
Skill:		
Knowledge:		

Briefly give one illustrative activity for the items that were integrated into the learning activity. If you indicated that any were omitted, explain why that happened.

_____

This alternate learning experience has (check all appropriate responses):

❏ provided qualifications for a career move or professional shift

❏ enhanced opportunities for advancement or promotion

❏ deepened depth and mastery of a specific professional expertise

❏ broadened career background for future professional repositioning

❏ tested abilities to start a business or consulting practice

❏ other.

1. Overall, how would you rate this learning experience and why?
   Excellent   Good   Fair   Poor

2. What, if anything, will you change in your professional continuing education plans based on this experience?

   _____

3. What, if anything, will you change in your PDP?

   _____

Chapter 9

Marketing Your Professional Strengths

To exist is to change, to change is to mature;
to mature is to go on creating oneself endlessly.

Henri Bergson

Knowing and accepting when to make changes in your work situation is the key to taking control of your career. Preparation prior to taking action is vital to making it happen effectively, efficiently, and with minimum stress. Most importantly, do not settle for your second or third choice of move or shift. Managing how you will conduct a successful work modification includes thinking about the "what ifs" and anticipating the development of a marketing strategy, including resources and tools necessary to take the next steps toward reaching your goal.

Now is the time to review how your career interests and priorities have changed. What are your emerging passions with respect to your present field? What do you see as the next challenge? The following career assessment exercise will help to compare your current work situation with your ideal one and identify critical gaps. Some basic questions to ask are

- Is my present job fulfilling and challenging work? Give reasons for responses.

- Considering ongoing changes in the T&D field, what job possibilities would now be of interest to me?

- Have I reached a point in my career when I should consider becoming an entrepreneur?

- Do I have competencies and expertise that I am not currently using, but want to? What type of work opportunities would allow me to use those capabilities?

- Would I want to use my skills and knowledge in a different type of organization or industry? Why?

- Are my present role and responsibilities meeting my expectations? Give reasons for the response.

- What part of my work am I passionate about? What do I dislike? What does this mean for a career move or professional shift?

- How can I best achieve my career mission and ultimate work goals?

Review your responses. What is your assessment of your career progress and employment situation? What are your thoughts regarding specific modifications you would like to have in your next work opportunity?

This chapter reviews essential items and activities needed to conduct a marketing campaign in a job search, for advancement, or for promoting yourself for business reasons. Changes and moves require knowing how you want to present yourself and what elements of your professional story to showcase for which audience.

Marketing Activities and Resources

Just as many other areas of your professional life have been affected by technology, new information, and trends, so too has your marketing and self-promotion changed. One of the best strategies for remaining professionally competitive is being in control of your career expansion and progress. Preparation is needed at all times, either to take advantage of unexpected opportunities by deliberately planning how to make a change in your work life, or to have the capability to handle unwelcome news, such as a layoff or downsizing. To ensure that you are prepared to market yourself, consider these questions:

- When was the last time you revised your résumé?

- Do you know what competencies or expertise you would want to showcase in a marketing campaign?

- Can you describe the professional image or brand you would like to project?

- Is your professional story up to date so that it represents the present to the future and not the past?

Your Product—Yourself

What AOEs, competencies, skills, knowledge, education, and achievements do you want to spotlight at the present time? Consider not only your experience in the T&D field, but also your transferable and adaptable skills. Identify the qualifications you want to use as well as those that will match a potential opportunity or position. Once more, refer to your PDP to keep on target about career goals and professional objectives, and be sure the information in a marketing document or presentation showcases the relevant components of your background. Take credit for what you have done. If you aren't in touch with yourself—strengths, weaknesses, and successes—you can't project the desired professional image and tell your professional story credibly and confidently. In other words, brag! Bragging is a necessity—not a choice—if you want to do more than just exist in a job; that is, be successful in your own eyes and to others. It isn't conceit; it is being forthcoming about who you are, what you have done, and what you are capable of doing. Peggy Klaus in *Brag!* states, "At its core, bragging is a very individual form of self-expression and communication" (2003).

Set a marketing objective that meets your needs, makes use of your background, details the type of role and responsibilities that you're enthusiastic about, shows the outcome or result you desire, and brings you closer to achieving your career vision.

Your Professional Niche

How much thought have you given to where you are presently positioned in the T&D field as compared to where you would like to be within the next three to five years? Think about the new trends or issues described in section I that could have an impact on your career journey and progress. Take another look at the revised AOEs that are now desirable, if not required, for success as a T&D specialist. You may need to rebundle or reprioritize your capabilities so that it's absolutely evident you have the qualifications to move ahead. Most likely, this will require rewriting the specifications of your professional niche to reflect how you currently want to promote yourself—the brand you want to create.

To create a demand for your expertise, you need to describe it in a brief marketing paragraph that serves as the basis for introducing yourself to new contacts or to renew old relationships. This marketing paragraph will help you develop a résumé; target your professional story for networking; transfer positions internally; or conduct an informational interview. You can then expand your customer or client base, persuade your supervisor you are ready for new responsibilities, or seek new employment. Most of all, you need to have "mojo," as defined by *Wikipedia* as one's self-confidence or self-esteem. It really matters the level or strength of belief in oneself in a situation. After all, without belief in yourself, how can you expect someone else to have confidence in you or your capabilities?

Develop Your Professional Story

Stories are the core of establishing your brand. They can be quite powerful in engaging people's attention to want to listen about you, or your products and services.

Select the appropriate elements or qualities for your story that stress advancing yourself in a highly visible way. Ask:
- Who should or who needs to hear my story?
- What is the reason for someone to listen to my story?
- How do I select which story to tell to each individual or group?
- How do I ensure that my story leads to desired outcomes?

All brands have carefully composed stories, projecting your passion, commitment, and authenticity of what you are marketing—these stories reinforce the bond. This action affects your success in achieving your goals. To ensure that you are telling the right story to the right audience, you need to stockpile various stories from which you can choose. These should be reviewed and updated regularly. You need to think of yourself as a storyteller and if you lack self-confidence, enroll in a workshop led by a professional storyteller.

This is Joanne's present dilemma: How to tell her story to convince people she is the most qualified person for the CLO position. This will be the key to marketing herself. Her story will need to project her passion about the power of learning and her leadership abilities. She may want to ask two or three of the CLOs she has met at her ASTD chapter to listen to her story and provide feedback.

Your Action Plan

Think of a marketing plan as a campaign: highly structured, practical, and organized. It should be realistic in terms of what you can add to your everyday schedule. Don't be overly ambitious about the tasks and activities that you can accomplish in a specific amount of time. Take into account your present job (if working), any professional development activities you're involved in, as well as personal and family commitments.

As a person just starting her T&D career, Lakshmi needs to develop a marketing mindset and truly think of herself as the product. The main obstacle she needs to overcome is her own shyness and lack of self-confidence. Creating an action plan will give Lakshmi a structured foundation from which to launch her job search campaign, and as she acts on her plan, she'll start to believe in herself.

First, spell out your marketing goals and the reasons for setting them. List the what, when, why, where, and how of the change or modification you want to happen in your work life. Basic elements to include are

- budget for costs involved, such as business cards, résumés, updated wardrobe
- priorities set up for order of tasks and actions—logical and practical
- to-do lists developed weekly with a completion time frame
- action plan timeline established for goal achievement.

As with your PDP, regularly review and revise your marketing action plan. Create activity tracking forms for such items as: networking follow-up meetings, people you need to contact or renew a relationship with, referral sources, and submission of résumés, applications, or certification documentation. Compare your activity tracking data with your plans. Don't be discouraged if you don't meet your benchmark for initiating this professional phase. Some events are out of your control, such as when a position opens up or the length of time required to start your own consulting practice.

Your Market

Whether you are seeking a new position, trying to advance within your present organization, increasing your client/customer base, or starting a business, you need to be knowledgeable about how local and regional economic, demographic, and business trends influence T&D practices in your location. Read the business section of your local newspapers (print or online) about growing community organizations, new start-up companies, and businesses moving into your area. If you are a coach, local demographics may determine the type of population growths leading you to expand your specializations, for example, adding retirement coaching, given the Boomer generation is increasingly entering their late 50s to early 60s. As a T&D specialist, if you learn that locally, assisted living housing has expanded or hospitals are enlarging their geriatric centers, you may want to transfer your expertise to these arenas. If you want to make moves or shifts where you're now working, read your organization's newsletter, and be part of the informal networking system and grapevine, particularly outside of your own section, to learn of potential areas of expansion, retirements, resignations, or promotions—which possibly open up job opportunities.

Determining your potential market allows you to tailor your professional story, résumé, or profile to showcase data and information that demonstrates how effectively you have the qualifications for a specific opening.

Using Marketing Strategies for Work Modifications and Movements

Using marketing strategies is relevant to various work situations and events, from convincing your supervisor that you are the one to lead a particular project, to giving a rationale for increasing your budget, to a presentation for a major potential new client. Given the purpose of this book, the focus is on marketing yourself for career growth and expansion purposes.

The rapid technological advancements have changed major procedures, resources, and tools of conducting a marketing campaign for the way you earn your living: in a new organizational position or when you initiate an independent practice. Think of yourself as a product that needs to be promoted in a very competitive market. How can you make your brand stand out? How can you make your message unique? Where should you be "tooting your own horn"?

The Internet as a Marketing Tool

Familiarity with the concept of social media is widespread. The majority of you most likely have an account with LinkedIn and Facebook and many people use Twitter—particularly the younger generations. The Internet has rapidly become an effective and efficient marketing tool. It has become the method of choice for assessing information for a job search: locating organizations, identifying recruiters, finding job listings, and posting résumés. This is the first place that job searchers turn to for data on industries, global opportunities, T&D specialties, and organizational staffing. You can also conduct an Internet search specific to your area and the types of employers that interest you. Any information you gather will help you target organizations or clients that potentially can use your capabilities and experience. You can distribute a résumé in a few minutes to numerous recruiters and employers.

How can you use the Internet to meet your marketing needs and your needs in seeking new opportunities? Use this resource to:

- learn more about the organizations that you would like to work for

- review organizations with positions that interest you

- identify specific job listings at an employer's website

- research resources and databases for the T&D field

- familiarize yourself with earnings and benefits norms and ranges

- find local networking events, coaches, résumé services, and recruiters

- examine differences in cost of living and other community information, if considering other geographic locations.

In addition to these reasons, the Internet is also an excellent broadcasting tool. Use an email blast with a résumé or professional profile attached to let colleagues, former classmates, members of your professional chapters, and networking groups know of your availability. In a brief paragraph, describe the type of work, organizations, or clients you are seeking. You can ask for leads, referrals, or ideas about resources for your next position. Note that you are available to meet to discuss your plans and interests.

The email blast would be a good strategy for Ric to tell everyone on his professional and personal listings about his situation and that he would welcome any support or suggestions. Opportunities may exist of which he isn't aware, and possible solutions can be recommended.

Websites are available to obtain career management resources, career advice, and coaching. You can participate in discussions, react to blogs, and gain support from other people seeking employment or contractual assignments. Establish your own blog as another way for people to find you. Using social media is today's way of broadcasting your brand and specific qualifications.

Social Media Tools

Being aware and actively using social media tools is a must for conducting a job search campaign. Social media mechanisms can expand and enhance your professional opportunities. Two important items you need to know before engaging in this communication mode:

- You should be clear about what qualifications and experience you want to offer.

- You should be able to tell your professional story and project your brand demonstrating your value.

The three big and popular social media tools are: LinkedIn, Facebook, and Twitter. Each offers advantages in your employment search or business expansion efforts.

- **LinkedIn:** The business-oriented social networking site. For professional networking whereby you link with others you wish to be associated with directly and indirectly. LinkedIn has special interest groups, allowing people to advance their careers by sharing expertise, experience, and knowledge. Groups exist for job searchers, T&D specialists, recruiters, professional organizations, and by generations, to mention a few—including ASTD. Locate them through LinkedIn's Groups Directory.

You should use LinkedIn to:
1. Expand professional brand visibility.
2. Build your industry or professional network.
3. Generate leads by responding to questions asked or comments made.
4. Identify potential employment opportunities.
5. Allow recruiters to find you via your key words, profile, or posted résumé.

- **Facebook:** Originally a place where people went to have fun, post photos, and meet friends, it's now changing and constructing a job search engine and related apps. Increasingly, more organizations are setting up a Facebook page.

- **Twitter:** As with Facebook, Twitter started strictly as a personal, fun method of staying in contact with family and friends. However, recently, employers have begun tweeting job listings, treating Twitter as a job board. The openings are disseminated through social media outlets. Apps are also available for use in your job search campaign.

Résumés

Although there have been many changes in the job search campaign tools, the résumé has always been and remains as your primary and important marketing document. However, the format, style, and way it's submitted have been revised and now make use of today's technology.

When was the last time you looked at your résumé? Is it so outdated that you have to start from scratch? As previously discussed, you are the product being marketed and your résumé presents your capabilities in an easy-to-read, focused, and targeted style. A résumé projects a professional image, introducing you in a concise, directed, clear, and individualized way. Think of it as the written version of your professional story. As a promotional piece, its main purpose is to spotlight your qualifications—strengths, professional savvy, and achievements—to be placed on the short list for a first-level interview.

Basically, you are putting together specific AOEs, competencies, skills, and experiences—that's your special brand, to showcase your unique professional niche in the workplace. A résumé doesn't have only one correct structure. You should create this document (not use a template), with your language and a format that's a fit for you. It should be kept updated and available.

Before developing your résumé, ask yourself the following questions:

- How can I package myself (as the product) to meet the needs of my present or future employer?
- What AOEs, competencies, skills, and knowledge do I want to spotlight?
- What technical and transferable qualifications do I have that are applicable to my T&D career and professional goals?
- What achievements and results demonstrate my capabilities and experiences?
- How can I illustrate my additional values to an employer?
- In what ways do I want to project my credibility and professionalism—standing out from my competition?
- How can I tell my story to be placed on the short list for a first-level interview or be considered for other professional opportunities?

The next consideration in résumé development is the technical process. Only if you are just starting out as a recent graduate with a bachelor's degree can your résumé be in a chronological format, one page in length. In this situation, you're marketing your potential value to an organization. Otherwise, you should develop a targeted functional résumé with a maximum length of two pages, highlighting your T&D and other qualifications, with key words and phrases that match a job or assignment qualifications, but that you feel truly represents your professional self.

Start with a powerful opening qualification summary or profile that summarizes your professional story. This is your "wow" declarative statement—the hook to grab a reader's attention—and is composed of your four or five most significant and impressive qualifications. The next section concentrates on the details and accomplishments of your T&D background and focuses on the professional savvy you bring to your work. You want people to believe that you can do exactly what they need you to do. The desired outcome of a résumé is that your professional story is told in an integrated way to leave a lasting impression.

If you feel your résumé needs a professional critique, use the services of a résumé consultant; your local ASTD Chapter may have résumé reviewers as part of its member career services. Or, look at the website of ASTD's Job Bank for its résumé review service.

Brief guidelines for scanning your résumé include

- familiarizing yourself with electronic technical procedures and guidelines, such as: ASCII or plain text format, recommended fonts, best email message subject strategies, and major differences between print and online résumés

- learning how employers and recruiters utilize scanners and résumé databases

- being prepared to complete an online application

- including accurate and specific action verbs and other information in your résumé or application that matches those used in a job description or assignment.

Professional Portfolios

Generally speaking, a portfolio allows you to showcase real examples of your accomplishments, stressing quality, creativity, professional breadth, and depth. It gives people the opportunity to see actual samples of your job performance results: needs assessments, training manuals, and surveys designed; analytical and evaluation reports submitted; measurement tools developed; project plans proposed; and so forth.

A portfolio doesn't replace a résumé; it presents your strongest assets as an additional marketing tool for promoting yourself. This is a way to include related examples from volunteer work, community service, and personal life that demonstrate the added value you bring to a situation. The flexibility of a portfolio allows specific accomplishments and skills to be grouped by focus, regardless of title, location, or date. Thus, a strong and highly visible image is given of your capabilities. It can be uploaded to your website, incorporated into a blog, or placed in your LinkedIn profile.

Kevin knows that he is a quality trainer and he is clearly interested in remaining in the field. He needs to regain his confidence and demonstrate his dedication, sincerity, and credibility. Creating a professional profile would enable him to illustrate (through concrete examples) the benefits of hiring a senior T&D specialist.

Networking and Opportunities

Networking is an organized and targeted process of developing contacts not only for job, contract, or client leads, but also for present or future sharing of resources, support, information, and ideas. Richard Bolles looks at these contacts or links as "bridge people" (2011). They bridge the gap between you and what you are seeking. Through networking you gain more visibility and increase your brand recognition.

These are some tips for successful networking:

- Understand that networking isn't informational interviewing, although that can be an outcome of networking.
- Know your networking goals clearly, such as seeking: job leads, new clients, contract leads, information about assessment tools, and professional learning options.
- Script an introduction that summarizes your needs, objectives, and some matching highlights of your story to generate credibility and interest.
- After introductions and some conversation, exchange business cards, and ask if you can call to schedule a follow-up meeting explaining your agenda concisely.
- Don't monopolize people's time, as they also want to meet other individuals.
- If the follow-up meeting results in a referral, inform the contact person of your actions and that an update will follow.

Take a long-term perspective on networking and stay in contact with people that you meet or with whom you have reconnected. You never know when the relationship you establish today will be just the contact you need tomorrow. The best places to expand your networking circle are the local chapters of human resources-related associations, local chamber of commerce, and other business and professional networking groups that can help you. Today, you are able to find groups for "professional women" and "generational" job seekers, both in real time and online.

Informational Interviewing

Informational interviewing gives you a real-life perspective—a quality unattainable from reading or viewing videos about the field. This is the opportunity to obtain answers from other T&D professionals doing the work that you want to do—whether you are considering a career in the field, looking for an entry-level position, planning to make a professional shift, assessing a different T&D specialization, or desiring to advance your career.

The goals of informational interviewing are to:

- Acquire useful information and resources.
- Obtain additional referrals and contact leads.
- Learn about relevant professional associations and other networking groups.
- Solicit advice or recommendations regarding your concerns and professional interests.

For informational interviews to be productive and not waste anyone's time, review the following tips:

- Reassure your interviewer that you aren't seeking a job.

- Acknowledge the person's time and set your appointment for 30 minutes.

- Email your résumé prior to the meeting (if interviewer doesn't already have it) as well as an agenda and sample questions.

- Take brief notes as questions are answered.

- Try to stay on course and not go off on a tangent.

- Questions should try to build a relationship and elicit the knowledge you seek.

- Follow up with an appreciative note or email.

To profit the most from this meeting, keep your questions focused, easy to follow, and don't collapse two or more topics into one question. Sample questions that you may want to ask include

- What are the challenges, trends, or critical arenas of T&D?

- What are the most important requirements to have for your role and responsibilities?

- As an independent consultant, what advice do you have for someone planning to start their own business?

- What professional degrees or credentials would be most helpful in qualifying for this area of expertise?

- What do you love the most about what you do? Why?

- What frustrates you the most? Why?

- What was your career progression? What are other viable options?

- How do you think my experience can help me succeed in making this career move or professional shift?

- As someone transitioning into the field, what are some steps that I can take to succeed in realizing my goal?

- Can you give me two other referrals that I may contact?

Readiness to Market Yourself

One of the best strategies for remaining professionally competitive and in control of your career is to anticipate the information and tools you should have. Are you ready to make your next work modification? Before meeting with anyone to discuss your future and before using any marketing document for networking or contact purposes, compile a checklist of tasks to ensure that you have completed all preparations. Turn to Exercise 9-1 to develop this checklist to track your tasks.

The final chapter stresses the importance of a long-term perspective, not only for professional survival, but also for a thriving, engaging, and meaningful T&D career.

Chapter Highlights

What have you learned? How can this information be applied to your career goals and professional dreams?

➤ What are the four basic questions a person should ask to determine if they are ready to begin a marketing campaign? Are you ready to initiate yours? Yes_____ No_____

➤ What are the four questions that determine what to include in a professional story? How can this input contribute to how you will market yourself?

➤ What are the six ways you can use the Internet to meet your marketing research needs? Check off those that would be most useful in your marketing strategy.

➤ What are the three most popular social media tools? Do you know how each one would be beneficial in your marketing campaign?

➤ What is a résumé "wow" declarative statement? Are you able to create yours? Yes_____ No_____
If not, what type of help will you seek?

➤ How would you define Richard Bolles' "bridge people"? Who are the bridge people in your network who can help you reach your career goals?

Exercise 9-1: The Marketing-Readiness Checklist

Directions: Indicate the completion status of each marketing or job search task that's relevant to you. Complete each task before beginning your marketing campaign.

Marketing or Job Search Task	Status		
	Complete	Incomplete	New Completion Date
Prepare a professional niche description portraying individualized combination of qualifications.			
Update my résumé or professional profile telling my professional story.			
Write a networking introductory script stating my needs and objectives (my "wow" statement).			
Create a fact sheet or capability statement showcasing strengths and achievements.			
Develop a job or type of service objective summarizing description of meaningful work.			
Establish LinkedIn and Facebook profiles, and a Twitter account.			
If independent (or planning to become one), create a webpage.			
Set up a plan of action for achieving marketing goals.			
Research and identify a database of clients or organizations with which I want to connect.			
Prepare for interviews, including informational ones, with an opening statement, a set of questions, a closing summary, and follow-up procedures.			
Establish a positive, confident mindset toward my campaign and activities.			

My marketing or job search campaign begins on _____.

Chapter 10

Managing for Professional Success

Live your dream by making deliberate choices,
not just responding to what life throws your way.

Marcia Wieder

Throughout the book, our message has been: Be prepared, ready, and accepting of change and of any unexpected, unanticipated opportunities. You have been given resources and tools to handle these situations with confidence and a belief in yourself. The underlying assumption is that complacency, "going with the flow," and believing that your job is secure can be your downfall. In addition, life circumstance changes will alter your professional needs, interests, and goals.

Because you never know when you'll be making a voluntary or forced career move or professional shift, it's important to take the following actions to maintain career success and achievement:

- Keep up to date with new work and societal developments, practices, and trends.
- Attend professional and networking sessions regularly.
- Conduct a full personal and professional self-review a minimum of once a year.
- Re-evaluate and update your PDP on a regular basis.

This chapter provides guidelines for your continuing success and survival, no matter what societal or business directions and concerns emerge, or how the T&D field and your career may evolve.

Challenges You Face

We've tried to envision the profession of the future based on present information and research. Section I has shown you how T&D is growing rapidly and expanding its borders. This reshaping will continue. The career model we've presented is likely to undergo future revisions due to the continuing effects of workplace trends, population changes, and the thinking of field experts. Ongoing activities, increasingly sophisticated use of social media, and new innovative technological tools will continue to strongly affect HRD departments and the way human resources business is conducted.

Furthermore, the field is still a popular one for career changers, who bring to T&D their specialized expertise and experience as well as up-to-date AOEs, competencies, and knowledge through their professional development and certification activities. They can provide stiff competition to experienced workers who haven't adapted to changes in the profession or taken advantage of lifelong learning options.

Taking into account the challenges you add into the mix, at the point in your career when you need to decide to continue to work or to retire (either part- or full-time), you should have career fluidity, have made career management a priority, maintained your brand visibility, and sustained career health.

Having Career Fluidity

One basic professional hurdle is having and retaining career fluidity—being adaptable to workplace innovations and realities. Don't lock your career into a rigid and motionless mode because job security hasn't existed for some time, and probably won't in the future. How do you remain flexible and ready to benefit from unexpected possibilities? How do you keep up with the broadening base of knowledge and technology? How do you stay competitive in the job market? Life is full of choices. You must be resolved in your choices and believe that your decisions are right for you at that moment in time.

For continual, ongoing professional success and engaging work, you must:

- Update your unique professional niche statement as needed.
- Determine when you need to move and what your next step will be.
- Target specific new expertise to gain that will strengthen your qualifications and move your career forward.
- Increase your organizational visibility and propose projects to meet employee needs, or volunteer for assignments that allow you to work across departments.
- Keep alert to new professional opportunities and innovative thinkers.
- Find time to continue your professional development in a way that works for you.

Taking care of these activities in a timely and effective manner strengthens your career fluidity. Keep control over your career path by using your PDP to stay on target and focused on your next task. The plan enables you to step back and notice any barriers that are the reasons for your career stagnation or the reasons you are being pulled in an unwanted direction. Being alert, prepared, ready, and having a positive attitude sustains career fluidity. It means that you are managing your professional life and determining your path toward your ideal career image.

Prioritizing Career Management

As busy as your life may be, it's essential that you include career and professional tasks on your priority list and integrate them in your daily planner. You are responsible for thinking ahead and acquiring the background to launch a viable and strong marketing operation when needed. Efficient and effective career management skills are a requirement for your survival and success in any work environment.

To prepare for PDP revisions, you should annually self-assess by completing a career or work check-up.

To learn your level of satisfaction with your present work situation, answer these questions:

- How closely does my present job match my ideal professional situation and what are the critical gaps?
- Am I still having fun?
- Do I still feel engaged by my work?
- Should I remain with this employer and look for career lattice opportunities to expand my horizons with new challenges, or is it time to initiate a career move or professional shift?

Your PDP is the cornerstone for career management. As discussed in chapter 6, a PDP is an evolving document that sets the path, pace, action plan strategies, and success milestones for your career progression. To see how you're doing managing your career, ask yourself these additional questions:

- Are you keeping to your scheduled interim success milestones for measurable accountability?

- Are you incorporating information from the interim milestone reviews and resulting adjustments in a yearly life management assessment?

If you have answered "yes" to both questions, your career management skills are fine and you can skip this section. However, responding "no" to both or either question may suggest poor career management. A "no" answer to the first may indicate that you're losing motivation and commitment to your long-term career goal, perhaps stemming from changes in your values, priorities, or interests. It can also be the result from interference due to an external event: a personal or family occurrence.

Good career management takes into account other aspects of your life that affect your career goals and professional plans, such as becoming a parent or needing to care for an ill relative. The last time you assessed your short-term PDP checkpoints, the consequences of a change may not have been apparent, but surfaced during a comprehensive review of where you are at this time in your life. Therefore, a PDP revisit may be called for due to these existing personal or professional circumstances.

Compile a list of the things that have occurred in your life within the last year. Check those that have affected or are now affecting your career and present work situation. Highlight those not considered in previous PDP adjustments and revisions and describe how and why their influence is significant. Now think of needed rescheduling, modifications, or revisions to your PDP as a result of these conditions. For example, if you didn't research coaching institutes as listed in your action plan, was it because of time limitations or a shift in your thinking about fulfilling work? If you recently became part of the sandwich generation (taking care of both young children and elderly parents), how does that affect your job or business? If you have new work responsibilities, do you feel the need for some additional training? Rethinking your career calling statement or perhaps rewriting your short-term career goals may be necessary for a better fit with the reality of what you can accomplish within the following year.

Exercise 10-1 will help you conduct an end-of-the year review and decide any additional PDP revisions that should be part of your good career management practices. To continue effectively managing your career, keep your sights on the tasks and activities on your to-do list between now and the next scheduled review of your PDP.

The challenge isn't only making career management a priority, but that it needs to become a natural routine. It's easy to get caught up with work deadlines as well as personal and family schedules and obligations. It's also easy to postpone career management tasks when other matters require your immediate attention and energy. Consider a time management workshop or seminar or hiring a coach to help you keep on target, be a sounding board, and motivate you to action.

Practice career management without giving much thought to whether you can or should be doing this. Adopt an attitude that's similar to the one you have for exercising, running errands, watching your weight, and carrying out other tasks. Do it automatically by posting tasks and activities on all your calendars—electronic and paper.

Keeping Your Brand Visible

An important component of staying ahead of your competition and being remembered by individuals is to maintain an up-to-date public presence. This is an essential feature of your career fluidity and survival. As you gain expertise, advance in your T&D career, expand consulting services, grow as a leader in the professional community, and add to your successes, you need to keep people informed of your latest activities.

Without awareness of your professional growth, development, achievements, and new experiences, you may not be remembered when flipping through a Rolodex for possible people to call for an opportunity or referral. In the other person's view, your professional brand will seem stagnant and your credibility weakened, thus diminishing your competitiveness.

To avoid this perception, review your professional image and niche statement on a regular basis to ensure they are current and think about how you want to market yourself right now. What changes are needed in your résumé's overall "wow" summary profile or in your qualifications list? How should you revise your networking intro statement? Does your business card or company brochure require a fresh new look? Updating a brand identity and thus your visibility renews your presence, giving you something to announce on your LinkedIn profile, blog, website, Facebook, and other social media sites.

Maintaining Career Health

Regard your career as you would your physical well-being. Similarly, you need to take preventive actions and do maintenance work. If you settle for your current status or rest on your laurels, your career is in danger of losing its fluidity and health that can lead to suffering burnout, losing the sense of challenge, or feeling you're in a rut. A most dire consequence would be the loss of your job.

These are some useful strategies for sustaining your career health:

- Retain harmony between your professional and personal lives.

- Build up positive energy toward your work.

- Keep your eye on what is most important to you.

- Avoid coasting along in your job or business and avoid taking shortcuts.

- Learn to manage stress before it manages you and your performance.

- Be alert to early warning signs that all is not well in your work world.

- Once you become aware that a change is required, embrace it as a challenge.

- Create your own interventions to enhance or redesign your position or business.

- Establish a professional file to track all achievements, contributions to the organization, professional activities, continuing professional development, and so forth.

- Anticipate future hurdles or difficulties and approach them head on.

- Listen to your own inner voice or intuition about your career.

Career health involves being mindful of your present work environment, status, and situation while being on the lookout for future possibilities and options. You should be ready for the unexpected opened window or possible brewing crisis. You know you can expect to work for several organizations or clients in various T&D roles and functions throughout your work life, thus, the following should be in place, ready to initiate at any time: marketing and your job search tools, resources, and strategies.

Long-Term Survival

Throughout this book we've emphasized the importance of taking responsibility for preparing and positioning yourself for career advancement. We can't predict exactly what will happen in the field in the next few years, but we can guarantee that organizations, industries, employment, and education will continue to be redefined and reshaped. We know that the transformation of T&D will continue. We definitely know that job security and career progression are passé. Survival and success rules have changed.

How is survival in the workplace now characterized? It's linked to your ability and confidence to bounce back and find a solution to a problem or issue. Career and job continuity occurs because you're willing and able to take risks, stay flexible, recover quickly from setbacks, explore options, and be accountable for your career moves and professional shifts.

Mentoring and Career Survival

In chapter 8, mentoring was discussed as an alternative means of professional development. It can also play an important role in raising your visibility within your organization and professional community. A mentor can help increase your chances of career survival by assisting you to understand company culture and its policies, to develop leadership skills, to become aware of the role and impact of the informal culture, to select reading materials, to make introductions to other key executives, and so forth. In seeking someone for this role, be sure that the person is willing to commit to being involved in a mentoring relationship.

Entrepreneurial Mindset

Achieving desired goals entails making choices, sometimes tough ones, and holding on to your power and persistence to cause things to happen for yourself. You can't assume that the competencies and experience you have today will serve you well tomorrow. A strong and confident mindset toward your work needs to be kept. Thinking of yourself as an entrepreneur maintains your competitive edge and determination. This is why lifelong career management—assessing, planning, implementing, and learning—is essential for professional growth and goal success. Before you can help your organization or clients achieve and sustain high performance, you need to have your own high performance track record.

Positioning yourself to profit from an opportunity calls for an entrepreneurial mindset, and that mindset is important whether you're internal or external to an organization. It helps you keep your career fluid and healthy, contributing to professional survival. An entrepreneurial mindset values the following behaviors:

- managing time and being organized

- having a vision and continually working to achieve it

- marketing and promoting yourself, your ideas, projects, clients, and customers

- speaking up and being assertive

- approaching problems creatively

- considering you're a leader

- meeting challenges straightforwardly

- being a self-disciplined self-starter

- believing in yourself and your abilities

- welcoming feedback and receiving criticism positively.

Your Professional Success

The last, but certainly not least, component of being strategic about your career is how you define professional success. This statement serves as a measurement of your place in the T&D profession.

How much time and energy do you give to your job? How much are you willing to give to a future job? Does it depend on whether you are working for someone else or for yourself? More to the point, how many years do you expect to work? If you're a typical worker, your answers probably are: "for a long time," "too long," or "even when I'm officially retired." Ideally, when the time has come for you to transition into full actual retirement and a new phase of your life, you'll feel that you've achieved professional success that was compatible with your values and sense of fulfilling and engaging work. That outcome would reflect a very skilled career manager indeed!

Only you can characterize what you consider to be professional success. As with your earlier definitions of fulfilling and engaging work (chapter 6), your values, priorities, and related changes you undergo during your work lifetime will influence your personal definition of professional success.

A professional success statement can combine many factors, including financial security, respect of colleagues, professional reputation, contribution to the field, job progression, reaching your full potential, employer's appreciation, integration of career and personal life, work engagement, status as a leader, and having your dream job. And at different points in your life, the meaning of professional success may change for you. Before exploring other work options, you should have a clear understanding of how you characterize success. Turn to Exercise 10-2 to develop your description of professional success.

In summary, we have given you a picture of what lies ahead for your T&D career and the resources for managing its direction and path. The responsibility for making your work life just "OK" or having it be your passion is dependent on you and your career management skills for now and the balance of the time you're in the workforce. Consider future changes and developments in this profession as the challenges and opportunities of a lifetime.

As you review the status of your work life, carefully study the revised ASTD Competency Model (chapters 2 and 3) and its implications for your direction and pathway. Be aware of how this model has redefined the field, with changes in AOEs such as Designing Learning to Instructional Design, Measuring and Evaluating to Evaluating Learning Impact, and Career Planning and Talent Management to Integrated Talent Management. A new AOE has been introduced: Learning Technologies. Several AOEs have a new focus such as mobile learning, social media, and learning analytics. Something new may grab your interest, or re-engage and re-energize you. Who knows what will be next? Having the knowledge and tools to direct your career and achieve your goals allows you to move or shift confidently when necessary and, most important, to create your distinctive course to personal and professional fulfillment.

Be a realistic optimist—combine a positive mindset with a measure of reality. No matter how many twists and turns your T&D career may take, follow your passion and remain enthusiastic. This will result in feeling you're making a difference to your employers, colleagues, and clients. Best of luck!

Chapter Highlights

What have you learned? How can this information be applied to your career goals and professional dreams?

➤ What are the four challenges that you face to experience continual success in the workplace? How do you believe you are handling these challenges?
Great____   Average____   Poorly____   Not at all____

➤ What are the six things you must do to have career fluidity? Do you have a strategy to keep your work engaging? Yes____   No____   Why? ____

➤ What are the four questions you need to ask to learn your work satisfaction level? How satisfied are you with your satisfaction level?
Very____   Medium____   Low____   Unsatisfactory____

➤ Identify a minimum of five of the 11 strategies listed for maintaining career health. How many are you missing to maintain your career health?

Exercise 10-1: Annual Review of Your Life Situation

Directions: Respond to the questions below. Think back over the last year about how satisfied you have been with your present life status and situation as compared to where you were the previous year. What events have affected your career and professional plans and consequently your PDP? What additional changes or adjustments will you need to make to your PDP? Answer questions that are relevant to your circumstances. If a question isn't applicable, indicate N/A.

Review of Your Personal and Family Life

1. List any major events that occurred within the past year (For example, joined the sandwich generation, became a parent, bought a new home). Describe the event(s) and the impact on your personal life including roles, relationships, and responsibilities.

   _____

2. Has your job been affected by the event (s)? If yes, describe the outcomes (for example: more stress, less travel, longer hours). If not, explain why not.

   _____

3. As a result of the event(s), was your PDP affected? If yes, list the sections (for example, long- or short-term goals, plan of action) that will need changes. Describe the revision(s) made. If not, explain why not.

   _____

4. Will you need to make any further changes or adjustments to your PDP for the coming year? Describe them.

   _____

5. Describe how you feel about the revisions to your PDP and the progress you hope to make toward achieving your goals.

   _____

Review of Your Professional Life

1. List any major events that happened within the past year (for example: promotion, relocation, termination). Describe the event(s) and the impact on your professional life including roles, relationships, and responsibilities.

   _____

2. Has your personal and home life been affected by the event(s)? If yes, describe the outcomes (for example, more anxiety and pressure, first-time travel, increased take-home work). If not, explain why not.

   _____

3. As a result of the event(s), was your PDP affected? If yes, list the sections (for example, long- or short-term goals, plan of action) that will need changes. Describe the revision(s) made. If not, explain why not.

   _____

4. Will you need to make any further changes or adjustments to your PDP for the coming year? Describe them.

   _____

5. Describe how you feel about the revisions to your PDP and the progress you hope to make toward achieving your goals.

   _____

6. In general, what are your hopes and practical expectations for this coming year?

   _____

Exercise 10-2: Defining Your Professional Success

Directions: Review the professional success factors and check off those that are important to you. Choose any number you wish. Then rank them in priority order, with 1 as the highest priority.

Professional Success Factors	Your Priority
Employer appreciation	
Ability to work at dream job	
Ability to work to fullest potential	
Manager's support	
Colleagues' respect	
Freedom to work independently	
Job advancement	
Desired income level	
Desired benefits	
Professional reputation	
Work-life balance	
Reputation as a leader	
Engaging or challenging work	
Can contribute to profession or field	
Other	

Write a brief statement that defines professional success for you. Include the above checked-off success factors and explain why they are important.

_____

_____

_____

_____

About the Authors

Caitlin Williams, PhD, is an author, speaker, trainer, and coach whose passion is bringing out the very best in the people she works with. Caitlin helps individuals and organizations identify opportunities to shine through improved performance, the demonstration of strengths, and the pursuit of making a difference in the world. Originally from Ohio, Caitlin spent the last eight years living and teaching in the Bay Area and Silicon Valley. She recently moved to Asheville, North Carolina, where she continues to coach and speak about workplace issues and about the value of focusing on strengths in work and in life.

Annabelle Reitman has more than 40 years of experience in career coaching and counseling, specializing in résumé development that targets clients' individualized professional stories as well as short-term coaching for people in work transitions, enabling them to successfully continue their career journey. Dr. Reitman is an established writer and author in the career and talent management arenas. Her latest publication is ASTD's *Infoline*, "Talent Engagement Across the Generations" (March 2013). She is co-author of a forthcoming coordinator's handbook for mentoring partnership programs, a model developed with Sylvia Benatti, to be published by ASTD Press in the spring of 2014. Since September 2009, Annabelle has been the Career Pathways columnist for The Transition Network (www.thetransitionnetwork.org). She is a past president and co-president of the ASTD Metro DC Chapter and past president of the Association of Career Professionals International (ACPI) DC Chapter. Annabelle served for six years as the coordinator of ACPI's online newsletter. For more than 25 years, she has conducted workshops at professional meetings and conferences. Dr. Reitman holds doctorate and master's degrees in higher education administration from Teachers College, Columbia University.

REFERENCES AND SUGGESTED READINGS

Ablow, D. (2012). "Why Cellphone Addiction Is Now on the Rehab Menu." Retrieved November 17, 2012 from www.foxnews.com/health/2012/09/21/why-mobile-phone-addiction-is-now-on-rehab-menu/.

Aducci, R., P. Bilderbeek, H. Brown, S. Dowling, N. Freedman, J. Gantz, A. Germanow, T. Manabe, A. Manfrediz, and S. Vema. (2008). "The Hyperconnected: Here They Come!" Framingham, MA: IDC.

Alboher, M. (2007). *One Person/Multiple Careers: The Original Guide to the Slash Career.* New York: Warner Books.

Alder Koten Staff. (2012). "Globalization 3.0 Is Here and It Will Change Your Career." Retrieved from www.alderkoten.com/ws/2011/06/globalization-3-0-change-career/.

Allen, C. (2011). "Burned Out and Fed Up? Maybe All You Need Is a Break." *T+D*. 65(12): 72.

Amabile, T., and S. Kramer. (2012). "How Leaders Kill Meaning at Work." *McKinsey Quarterly*. Retrieved August 29, 2012 from www.mckinseyquarterly.com/How_leaders_kill_meaning_at_work_2910.

———. (2012). "What Makes Work Worth Doing?" HBR Blog Network. Retrieved September 4, 2012 from http://blogs.hbr.org/hbsfaculty/2012/08/what-makes-work-worth-doing.html.

———. (2011). *The Progress Principle: Using Small Wins to Ignite Joy, Engagement, and Creativity at Work.* Boston: Harvard Business School Press.

Andrusia, D., and R. Haskins. (2000). *Brand Yourself.* New York: Ballantine Publishing Corp.

Aon Hewitt. (2012). 2012 *Trends in Global Employee Engagement.* Retrieved February 14, 2013 from www.aon.com/human-capital-consulting/thought-leadership/leadership/2012_Trends_in_Global_Employee_Engagement.jsp.

Apollo Research Institute. (2012). *The Future of Work Report.* Phoenix, AZ: Apollo Group, Inc.

Arneson, J., W. Rothwell, and J. Naughton. (2013). "Training and Development Competencies: Redefined to Create Competitive Advantage." *T+D*. (67)1: 42-47.

———. *(2013). ASTD Competency Study: The Training & Development Profession Redefined.* Alexandria, VA: ASTD Press.

Arruda, W., and K. Dixson. (2007). *Career Distinction: Stand Out by Building Your Brand.* Hoboken, NJ: John Wiley & Sons.

ASTD Career Development Community. (2012). "Bridging the Skills Gap: Help Wanted, Skills Lacking: Why the Mismatch in Today's Economy?" Alexandria, VA: ASTD.

ASTD Research. (2012). *The Global Workplace: Learning Beyond Borders*. 4(2). Alexandria, VA: ASTD Press.

ASTD Staff. (2012). "Five Workplace Trends." Retrieved February 14, 2013 from www.astd.org/Publications/Blogs/ASTD-Blog/2012/04/Five-Workplace-Trends.

Austin, G. (2012). "Is It Time for Asperger's in the Workplace?" *Profiles in Diversity Journal* 14(6): 60-61.

Avey, C. (2013). "What Can You Expect in 2013?" *Chief Learning Officer*. 12(1): 26-47.

Beck, M. (2010). "Mind Games: Attention-Deficit Isn't Just for Kids." *The Wall Street Journal*. Retrieved February 13, 2013 from online.wsj.com/article/SB1000142405270230462030457516590293305 9076.html.

Benko, C., and A. Liakopolos. (2011). "The Corporate Lattice." *Talent Management*. 7(2): 28-31.

Biech, E., ed. (2008). *ASTD Handbook for Workplace Learning Professionals*. Alexandria, VA: ASTD Press.

Bingham, T., and P. Galagan. (2011). "Committed to Innovation." *T+D*. 65(7): 32-37.

Bolles, M., and R. Bolles. (2011). *What Color Is Your Parachute? Guide to Job-Hunting Online*. Berkeley, CA: Ten Speed Press.

Bolles, R. (2013). *What Color Is Your Parachute?* Berkeley, CA: Ten Speed Press.

Boudreau, A. (2011). "The Next Boomer Bonanza." *Profit*. 30(8): 7-8.

Bridges, W. (1995). *JobShift: How to Prosper in a Workplace Without Jobs*. Cambridge, MA: Da Capo Press.

Briggs, B. (2012). "Veteran Unemployment Rate Dips, But Crisis Deepens for Ex-Military Women." Retrieved February 1, 2013 from usnews.nbcnews.com/_news/2012/10/05/14244058-veteran-unemployment-rate-dips-but-crisis-deepens-for-ex-military-women?lite.

Buckingham, M. (2011). *StandOut*. Nashville, TN: Thomas Nelson.

Calling Brands. (2012). *Crunch Time: Why We Need Purpose at Work*. London, UK: Calling Brands.

Campbell, J., and W. Finegan. (2011). "Dawn of the Social Cyborg." *Training Magazine*. 48(5): 20-27.

Caruso, C., L. Charles, T. Lawson, A. Nkata, K. Sieber, S. Pandalai, and R. Hitchcock. (March 2012). NIOSH *Research on Work Schedules and Work-Related Sleep Loss*. Retrieved from http://blogs.cdc.gov/niosh-science-blog/2012/03/09/sleep/.

Casey, C., and Deloitte & Touche. (2010). "Traditionalists, Baby Boomers, Generation X, Generation Y (and Generation Z) Working Together." United Nations Joint Staff Pension Fund. Retrieved February 5, 2013 from www.un.org/staffdevelopment/pdf/Designing%20 Recruitment,%20Selection%20&%20Talent%20Management%20Model%20tailored%20 to%20meet%20UNJSPF's%20Business%20Development%20Needs.pdf.

Castellano, S. (2012). "Going Global." *T+D*. 66(10): 15.

Catalyst. (2012). "Lesbian, Gay, Bisexual, and Transgender Workplace Issues." New York: Catalyst.

Chritton, S. (2012). *Personal Branding for Dummies*. Hoboken, NJ: John Wiley & Sons.

Cleaver, J. (2012). *The Career Lattice: Combat Brain Drain, Improve Company Culture, and Attract Top Talent*. New York: McGraw Hill.

Collamer, N. (2013). *Second-Act Careers*. Berkeley, CA: Ten Speed Press.

Collins Brewer, L. (2011). "The Professional Pigeonhole: How to Escape and Expand Your Career Options." *T+D*. 65(1): 70-71.

Corner, J. (2012). "Tech-Infused Mentoring." *T+D*. 66(6): 50-53.

Cornish, E. (2011). "Connectivity and Its Discontents: Book Review of Alone Together." *The Futurist*. 55(4): 53.

——. (2010). "Foresight Conquers Fear of the Future." *The Futurist*. 47(1): 50-51.

——. (2012). *The Futurist*.

Cowan, R. (2010). "Ten Ways to Measure Learning Impact." *Links Plus*. Alexandria, VA: ASTD.

D'Mello, S. (2012). *Stress: The Global Economic Downturn Has Taken Its Toll on Employees*. A 2011/2012 Kenexa High Performance Institute Worktrends Report. Retrieved February 5, 2013 from http://khpi.com/Current-R-D/WorkTrends/Stress.

Davis, A., D. Fidler, and M. Gorbis. (2011). *Future Work Skills 2020*. Retrieved November 12, 2012 from http://apolloresearchinstitute.com/sites/default/files/future_work_skills_2020_ full_research_report_final_1.pdf.

Dudley, D. (2010). "We Need to Talk". *AARP Magazine*. March-April: 65-68.

Dunnett, R. (2012). "Bring Your Own Device." *Director*. 65(9).

Duffy, J. (2008). "16% of Workers Across the World Are 'Hyperconnected.'" Retrieved December 2, 2012 from www.networkworld.com/news/2008/051408-hyperconnected-study.html.

Dychtwald, K., T.J. Erickson, and R. Morison. (2006). *Workforce Crisis: How to Beat the Coming Shortage of Skills and Talent*. Boston: Harvard Business School Press.

Ellis. S. (2004). *The Volunteer Recruitment (and Membership Development) Book*. Philadelphia, PA: Energize, Inc.

——. (undated). "Why Volunteer?" Retrieved March 3, 2013 from http://energizeinc.com/art/ awhy.html.

Emelo, R. (2011). "Creating a New Mindset: Guidelines for Mentorship in Today's Workplace." *T+D.* 65(1): 44-48.

———. (2012). "Mentoring in the Networked Workplace." *Talent Management.* 8(4): 26-29.

Ensher, E., and S. Murphy. (2005). *Power Mentoring: How Successful Mentors and Protégés Get the Most Out of Their Relationships.* San Francisco, CA: Jossey-Bass.

ERC Insights Blog. (2012). "Employers Facing Retention Challenges." Retrieved February 9, 2013 from www.yourerc.com/blog/post/Employers-Facing-Retention-Challenges.aspx.

———. (2012). "Employers Attempt to Identify Retention Challenges." Retrieved February 9, 2013 from www.yourerc.com/blog/post/Employers-Raise-Concerns-as-Training-Efforts-Stagnate.aspx.

Feller, R., and J. Whichard. (2005). *Knowledge Nomads and the Nervously Employed: Workplace Change and Courageous Career Choices.* Austin, TX: PRO-ED.

Ferguson, M. (2011). "How American Business Can Navigate the Skills Gap." Retrieved February 5, 2013 from http://blogs.hbr.org/cs/2011/11/how_american_business_can_navi.html.

Fieldstein, M. (2012). "Are You Building Strong Career Relationships?" *T+D.* 66(12): 72-73.

Floro, N. (2011). "Mobile Learning." *Infoline,* 28(1110). Alexandria, VA: ASTD Press.

Franko, A. (2012). "Workplace Learning and Development: A Driving Force for Innovation." Retrieved from www.astd.org/Publications/Newsletters/ASTD-Links-Articles/2012/10/A-Driving-Force-for-Innovation.html.

Friedman, T. (2005). *The World Is Flat.* New York: Farrar, Straus and Giroux.

———. (2012). "If You've Got the Skills, She's Got the Job." *The New York Times.* Retrieved from www.nytimes.com/2012/11/18/opinion/sunday/Friedman-You-Got-The-Skills.html?_r=0.

Friedman, T., and M. Mandelbaum. (2011). *That Used to Be Us: How America Fell Behind in the World It Invented and How We Can Come Back.* New York: Farrar, Straus and Giroux.

Galagan, P. (2012). "Amplified and Connected." *T+D.* 66(12): 34-37.

———. (2012). "From Pie in the Sky to the Palm of Your Hand: The Proliferation of Devices Spurs More Mobile Learning." *T+D.* 66(3): 29-31.

———. (2012). "How Would You Train a Transhuman?" *T+D.* 66(1): 27-29.

———. (2009). "Dude, How'd I Do?" *T+D.* 63(7): 24-26.

Gallagher, J., K. Young, A. Meyer, and S. Tompor. (2012). "6 Challenges Affecting the American Worker." *USA Today.* Retrieved October 25, 2012 from http://usatoday30.usatoday.com/news/nation/story/2012-09-03/challenges-facing-workers/57541098/1.

Garff, M. (2012). "Take on the Talent Crisis: Accenture Offers Six Strategies for Organizations Struggling to Fill a Skills Gap. *T+D.* 66(2): 21.

Global Workplace Analytics. (June 2011). "The State of Telework in the U.S. – Five-Year Trend and Forecast." Retrieved February 1, 2013 from www.globalworkplaceanalytics.com/whitepapers.

Globoforce. (2011) *Workforce Mood Tracker Reveals Misalignment Between Employee Recognition and Performance.* Retrieved February 14, 2013 from www.globoforce.com/mood-tracker-april-2011-report.

Godin, S. (2010). *Linchpin: Are You Indispensable?* New York: Penguin Group.

Goldsmith, M. (2012). "Are You Surviving or Succeeding?" *Talent Management.* 8(8): 50.

———. (2011). "Who Do People Think You Are?" *Talent Management.* 7(2): 50.

———. (2007). *What Got You Here Won't Get You There: How Successful People Become Even More Successful.* New York: Hyperion.

Gordon, E.E. (2012). "The Global Talent Chase: China, India, and U.S. Vie for Skilled Workers." *The Futurist.* 46(6): 43-47.

Greenhouse, S. (2008). *The Big Squeeze: Tough Times for the American Worker.* New York: Alfred A. Knopf.

Gurchiek, K. (2011). "Look for Global, Rather Than Cross-Cultural, Perspectives." *HR Magazine.* 56(11): 89.

———. (2009). "Motivating Innovation." *HR Magazine.* 54(9): 31–35.

Haneberg, L. (2011). "Training for Agility: Building the Skills Employees Need to Zig and Zag." *T+D.* 65(9): 50-54, 56.

Hankin, H. (2005). *The New Workforce: Five Sweeping Trends That Will Shape Your Company's Future.* New York: AMACOM.

Hannon, K. (2010). *What's Next? Follow Your Passion and Find Your Dream Job.* San Francisco, CA: Chronicle Books.

Harkness, H. (2008). "The Yo-Yo Model for Your Future Career: You're on Your Own." *Career Planning and Adult Development Journal* 24(2): 10–21.

Hastings, R. (2012). "Multilingual Skills, Cultural Understanding Rise in Importance." *HR Magazine.* 57(10): 20.

Hecklinger, F., and B. Black. (2010). *Training for Life.* Dubuque, IA: Kendall/Hunt Publishing.

Herman Trend Alert. (2012). "The New Geography of Talent." Retrieved August 29, 2012 from http://www.hermangroup.com/alert/archive_8-29-2012.html.

———. (2012). "Numbers of Older Workers Will Soon Exceed Younger Workers." Retrieved November 17, 2012 from www.hermangroup.com/alert/archive_7-11-2012.html.

———. (2012). "Purpose Emerging as Important Driver of Engagement." Retrieved November 17, 2012 from www.hermangroup.com/alert/archive_5-16-2012.html.

——. (2012). "U.S. Playing Catch-Up." Retrieved January 26, 2012 from www.hermangroup.com/alert/archive_1-25-2012.html.

——. (2011). "Flexibility – Increasingly Important Benefit." Retrieved November 17, 2012 from www.hermangroup.com/alert/archive_2-23-2011.html.

——. (2011). "Employee Loyalty Declines Worldwide." Retrieved November 20, 2011 from www.hermangroup.com/alert/archive_11-16-2011.html.

Herring, S., and P. Galagan. (2011). "Why Innovation? Why Now?" *T+D*. 65(9): 26-28.

Herrmann-Nehdi, A. (2010). "Whole Brain Thinking: Ignore It at Your Peril." *T+D*. 64(5): 36-41.

Hobson, K. (2009). "Why Your Job May Be Killing You." *U.S. News & World Report*.

Hoffman, R., and B. Casnocha. (2012). *The Start Up of You*. New York: Crown Business.

Insured Retirement Institute. (2012). *Retirement Readiness of Generation X: An Overview of the Next Generation of Retirement Investors*. Retrieved from https://myirionline.org/eweb/uploads/research/Gen%20X%20FINAL.pdf.

Jobvite. (2011). "Social Job Seeker Survey." Retrieved January 30, 2012 from http://web.jobvite.com/rs/jobvite/images/Jobvite-Social-Job-Seeker-Survey-2011.pdf.

Joerres, J. (2011). "A New Era Is Upon Us—the Human Age." Retrieved from manpowergroup.com/humanage.

Jones, C. (2012). "Sour Economy Gives Rise to Extreme Commuters." *USA Today*. Retrieved from http://travel.usatoday.com/news/story/2012-08-16/Sour-economy-gives-rise-to-extreme-commuters/57099694/1.

Kalman, F. (2013). "Has Executive Education Gone Soft?" *Chief Learning Officer*. 12(1): 18-21.

Kaye, B. (2011). "Up Is Not the Only Way…Really!" *T+D*. 65(9): 40-45.

Kaye, B, and J.W. Giulioni, J. W. (2012). *Help Them Grow or Watch Them Go: Career Conversations Employees Want*. San Francisco: Berrett-Koehler Publishers.

——. (2012). "Lose the Career Ladder and Hit the Wall." *T+D*. 66(9): 44-47.

Ketter, P. (2012). "Embrace Change." *T+D*. 66(12): 10.

——. (2010). "How the Brain Learns…" *T+D*. 64(5): 10.

Kellogg, V. (2008). "Job Worries Have a Name: 'Recession Rumination.'" *USA Today*. Retrieved from http://newyork.newsday.com/entertainment/tv/inside-long-island-business-1.811933/job-worries-have-a-name-recession-rumination-1.816479.

Klaus, P. (2003). *Brag! The Art of Tooting Your Own Horn Without Blowing It*. New York: Warner Books.

Krell, E. (2012). "Expats: Keeping Feet in Two Cultures." *HR Magazine*. Retrieved February 14,

2013 from https://www.shrm.org/Publications/hrmagazine/EditorialContent/2012/1212/Pages/1212-cultural-integration-skills.aspx.

Kruger, P. (2012). "Nearly Half of College-Educated Workers Are Overqualified for Their Jobs." Retrieved January 29, 2013 from http://jobs.aol.com/articles/2013/01/28/college-educated-over-qualified-study/?icid=maing-grid7%Cmaing8%/html.

Leahy, C. (2012). "The Workforce of the Future: Older and Healthier." *Fortune*. Retrieved from http://management.fortune.cnn.com/2012/01/09/workforce-future-older/.

Lesonsky, R. (2012). "Can't Give Raises This Year? Try Training Instead." Retrieved February 14, 2013 from www.openforum.com/articles/cant-give-raises-this-year-try-training-instead/.

Levit, A. (2012). *Retention Coaching*. Retrieved February 9, 2013 from www.astd.org/Publications/Blogs/Learning-Executive-Blog/2012/09/Retention-Coach.

———. (2011). *Using Social Media to 'Net' a Job*. Northfield, MN: Life Skills, (#7046).

Looper, L. (n.d.). "How Generation Z Works." Retrieved January 14, 2013 from http://people.howstuffworks.com/culture-traditions/generation-gaps/generation-z.htm.

Lore, N. (2011). *The Pathfinder*. New York: Touchstone.

Lorenz, M. (2012). "Younger Bosses: The New Normal?" Retrieved January 10, 2013 from http://thehiringsite.careerbuilder.com/2012/09/13/younger-bosses-the-new-normal/little-economist/.

Lucas, B. (2008). "Brain-Based Learning." Retrieved February 12, 2013 from www.astd.org/Publications/Newsletters/ASTD-Links/ASTD-Links-Articles/2008/04/.

Madell, R. (2012). "LGBT: Progress and Problems in the Workplace, Part 1." Retrieved January 13, 2013 from www.theglasshammer.com/news/2012/06/25/lgbt-progress-and-problems-in-the-workplace-part-1/12).

Malamed, C. (2013). "Learning Technology Trends to Watch in 2012." *The eLearning Coach: Tips and Reviews for Success With Online and Mobile Learning*. Retrieved from http://theelearningcoach.com/elearning2.0/learning-technology-trends-for-2012/.

Masie, E. (2013). "The Future of Mobile Learning." *Chief Learning Officer* online. Retrieved January 2, 2013 from http://clomedia.com/articles/view/the-future-of-mobile-learning.

———. (2012). "Learning Intensity, Introverts in the Workplace." *Elliott Masie's Learning TRENDS*. Retrieved January 6, 2013 from http://trends.masie.com/archives/2012/10/15/754-learning-intensity-introverts-in-the-workplace.html.

———. (2012). "Taking the Train, Huge Learning Options, Last-Minute Choices." *Elliott Masie's Learning TRENDS*. Retrieved from http://trends.masie.com/archives/2012/10/11/753-taking-the-train-huge-learning-options-last-minute-choic.html.

———. (2012). "Temp Workers & Training, Whiteboards, Oh Myyy From George Takei." *Elliott Masie's Learning TRENDS*. Retrieved February 5, 2013 from http://trends.masie.com/archives/2012/9/18/745-temp-workers-training-whiteboards-oh-myyy-from-george-ta.html.

——. (2012). "Video Role in Learning Grows." *Elliott Masie's Learning TRENDS.* Retrieved January 6, 2013 from http://trends.masie.com/archives/2013/1/3/video-role-in-learning-grows.html.

Mattioli, D. (2009). "With Fewer U.S. Opportunities, Home Looks Appealing to Expats." *The Wall Street Journal.* Retrieved January 4, 2010 from http://online.wsj.com/article/SB100014 24052748704869304574595831070819244.html.

Maxwell, J. (2008). *Mentoring 101.* Nashville, TN: Thomas Nelson.

McCool, J.D. (2012). *2012 Executive Job Market Intelligence Report.* Retrieved February 14, 2013 from www.execunet.com/e_trends_survey.cfm.

McGraw, M. (2012). "Where's Gen Y Going to Work (and Why)?" *Human Resource Executive Online.* Retrieved September 11, 2012 from www.hreonline.com/HRE/view/story.jhtml?id=533350574.

Meinert, D. (2012). Sleepless in Seattle…and Cincinnati and Syracuse." *HR Magazine.* 57(10): 54-58.

——. (2012). "Hidden Wounds." *HR Magazine.* 56(7): 24-29.

Meister, J.C., and K. Willyerd (2010). *The 2020 Workplace: How Innovative Companies Attract, Develop, and Keep Tomorrow's Employees Today.* New York: HarperCollins Publishers.

Middleton, J., K. Langdon, and N. Cartwright. (2007). *Land Your Dream Job.* New York: Penguin Group.

Miller, S. (2012). "LGBT Employees Face Retirement Challenges." SHRM. Retrieved January 24, 2013 from www.shrm.org/hrdisciplines/benefits/Articles/Pages/LGBT-Employees-Retirement.aspx.

MindTools. (2013). "Creating a Value Proposition." Retrieved February 5, 2013 from http://www.mindtools.com/CommSkll/ValueProposition.htm.

Minton-Eversole, T. (2012). "Virtual Teams Used Most By Global Organizations, Survey Says." SHRM. Retrieved February 1, 2013 from www.shrm.org/hrdisciplines/orgempdev/articles/pages/virtualteamsusedmostbyglobalorganizations.surveysays.aspx

Mourshed, M., D. Farrell, and D. Barton. (2012). *Education to Employment: Designing a System That Works.* McKinsey & Company. Retrieved February 14, 2013 from: http://mckinseyonsociety.com/education-to-employment/report/.

Murphy. E., and E. Erisher. (2006). "Establishing a Great Mentoring Relationship." *T+D.* 60(7): 27-28.

Natchez, M. (2012). "Clout: How to Be the One Who Has It." *T+D.* 66(7): 72-73.

Neittlich, A. (2012). "10 Signs You Might Be an Excellent Coach." *T+D.* 66(11): 70-73.

Noerr, D. M. (2009). *Healing the Wounds: Overcoming the Trauma of Layoffs and Revitalizing Downsized Organizations.* New York: John Wiley & Sons.

Norris, F. (2012). "The Number of Those Working Past 65 Is at a Record High." *The Wall Street Journal*. Retrieved January 21, 2013 from www.nytimes.com/2012/05/19/business/economy/number-of-those-working-past-65-is-at-a-record-high.html?_r=0.

NOVA Workforce Development. (2012). *NOVA Board: Digital Literacy Skills Essential for Access & Advancement in 21st Century Global Economy*. Retrieved February 12, 2013 from http://novaworks.org/Portals/3/Nova/Docs/Board/DigitalLiteracy_100812.pdf.

Oakes, K., and P. Galagan, eds. (2011). *The Executive Guide to Integrated Talent Management*. Alexandria, VA: ASTD Press.

Oxford Economics and Towers Watson. (2012). *Global Talent 2021: How the New Geography of Talent Will Transform Human Resource Strategies*. Retrieved January 31, 2013 from www.towerswatson.com/assets/pdf/7656/Global_talent_2021.pdf.

Pace, A. (2012). "Preparing Today's Youths for Tomorrow's Workplace." *T+D*. 66(12): 42-46.

Pandya, C. (2012). "Limited English Proficient Workers and the Workforce Investment Act: Challenges and Opportunities." Migration Information Source. Retrieved January 13, 2013 from www.migrationinformation.org/Feature/display.cfm?ID=900.

Pelan, V. (2012). "The Difference Between Mentoring and Coaching." *Talent Management*. 8(2): 34-37.

Peters. L. (1994). *The Pursuit of Wow!* New York: Vintage Books.

Pink, D. (2011). *Drive: The Surprising Truth About What Motivates Us*. New York: Riverhead Books.

Pirie, C. (2012). "Technology + Learning = Inspiration." *T+D*. 66(12): 38-41.

Price, M., R. Herod, and C. Burns-Green. (2012). "Mercer's 2011-2012 Benefits Survey for Expatriates and Internationally Mobile Employees." Retrieved from www.imercer.com/expatbenefits.

Prudential. (2012). *The LGBT Financial Experience*. Retrieved January 24, 2013 from www.prudential.com/view/page/public/30500.

PwC Saratoga. (2012). *PwC Saratoga 2011/2012 U.S. Human Capital Effectiveness Report*. Retrieved February 9, 2013 from www.pwc.com/us/en/hr-saratoga/publications/human-capital-effectiveness-report.jhtml.

Quittner, J. (2013). "The Challenges of Hiring Recent Veterans." *Inc*. Retrieved February 5, 2013 from www.inc.com/magazine/201302/jeremy-quittner/the-challenges-of-hiring-recent-veterans.html.

Ramsey, S.J., and B. Schaetti. (1999). "Reentry: Coming 'Home' to the Unfamiliar: Repatriates May Feel Like Strangers in a Strange Land." Retrieved from www.transition-dynamics.com/reentry.html.

Rath, T. (2007). *StrengthsFinder 2.0*. New York: Gallup Press.

Reitman, A. (2013). "Talent Engagement Across Generations." *Infoline*, no. 1303. Alexandria, VA: ASTD Press.

Rock, D. (2011). "The 'Aha' Moment." *T+D.* 65(2): 45-49.

Rosenberg, A. (2009). *101 Ways to Stand Out at Work.* Avon, MA: Adams Media.

Rossheim, J. (2012). "Tapping Retirees for Contingent Workforce Needs." Retrieved August 8, 2012 from http://hiring.monster.com/hr/hr-best-practices/recruiting-hiring-advice/strategic-workforce-planning/contingent-workforce.aspx.

Rothwell, W.J. (2012). "13 Practical Tips for Training in Other Countries." *T+D.* 66(5): 39-41.

Rothwell, W.J., and J.M. Graber. (2010). *Competency-Based Training Basics.* Alexandria, VA: ASTD Press.

Rothwell W.J., H.L. Sterns, D. Spokus, and J.M. Reaser. (2008). *Working Longer: New Strategies for Managing, Training, and Retaining Older Employees.* New York: AMACOM.

Schawbel, D. (2012). "Career Strategies: How Different Generations of Americans Try to Find Work." *Time: Business & Money* online column. Retrieved from http://business.time.com/2012/09/24/how-different-generations-of-americans-try-to-find-work/.

Schepp, D. (2011). "Many American Workers Afraid to Take Vacation." Retrieved December 2, 2012 from http://jobs.aol.com/articles/2011/07/08/many-american-workers-afraid-to-take-vacation/.

Schramm, J. (2012). "Tomorrow's Workforce." *HR Magazine.* 57(3): 112.

——. (2011). "Arrested Development." *HR Magazine.* 56(8): 104.

Sheridan, K. (2012). *Building a Magnetic Culture.* New York: McGraw Hill.

SHRM. (2010). *Employing Military Personnel and Recruiting Veterans: What HR Can Do.* www.shrm.org/research/surveyfindings/documents/10-0531%20military%20program%20report_fnl.pdf.

Solutions Design. (2009). "The Power of 4: The Four Generations: Who They Are." Indianapolis, IN: ADAYANA.

Sullivan, J. (2012). "VUCA: The New Normal for Talent Management and Workforce Planning." Retrieved December 22, 2012 from www.ere.net/2012/01/16/vuca-the-new-normal-for-talent-managent-and-workforce-planning/.

SumTotal Systems. (2012). "Mid-Year Checkpoint: Top Learning Trends for 2012." Retrieved February 1, 2013 from www.ihrimpublications.com/white_papers/SumTotal_White_Paper-Mid-Year_Checkpoint.pdf.

Szeltner, M., C. Van Horn, and C. Zukin. (2013). *Diminished Lives and Futures: A Portrait of America in the Great-Recession Era.* New Brunswick, NJ: Rutgers University Heldrich Center. Retrieved February 1, 2013 from www.heldrich.rutgers.edu/sites/default/files/content/Work_Trends_February_2013.pdf.

Tandon, Y. (February, 2012). "Why Work-Life Balance Isn't Balanced." *Gallup Management Journal.* Retrieved February 9, 2012 from http://gmj.gallup.com.

Thilmany, J. (2008). "Passing on Know-How." *HR Magazine.* 53(6).

Tsufit. (2008). *Step Into the Spotlight*. Canada: Beach View Books.

Tucker, M. (2011). "Don't Say Goodbye." *HR Magazine*. 56(8): 71-73.

Turkle, S. (2011). *Alone Together: Why We Expect More From Technology and Less From Each Other*. New York: Basic Books.

U.S. Department of Labor (2012). "A Profile of the Working Poor, 2010." Report 1035.

Vanderkam, L. (2011). *168 Hours: You Have More Time Than You Think*. New York: Penguin.

Waldman, J. (2011). *Job Search With Social Media for Dummies*. Hoboken, NJ: John Wiley & Sons.

Wikipedia. (2013). "M-learning." Retrieved from http://en.wikipedia.org/wiki/M-learning.

Williams, A. (2012). "Just Wait Until Your Mother Gets Home." *The New York Times*. Retrieved January 24, 2013 from www.nytimes.com/2012/08/12/fashion/dads-are-taking-over-as-full-time-parents.html?pagewanted=all.

Williams, C. (2009). "The Working Worried: How Career Development Practitioners Can Help." Retrieved February 5, 2013 from ncda.org/aws/NCDA/pt/sd/news_article/21850/_PARENT/layout_details_cc/false.

——. (2013). Personal interview with Lorelle Swader.

——. (2013). Personal interview with Sylvia Benatti.

——. (2013). Personal interview with Lynn Ware.

——. (2013). Personal interview with Connie Malamed.

Wlson, C. (2012). "When Opportunity Knocks, Can You Walk the Talk?" *T+D*. 66(6): 72-73.

Wilson, M., and L. Mohl. (2012). *Networking Is Dead: Making Connections That Matter*. Dallas, TX: BenBella Books.

Withers, B. (2009). "Creating the Feedback Partnership." *T+D*. 63(3): 78-79.

WorldatWork (2007). "Flexibility a Matter of Culture, Experts Say." Presentation at Work-Life 2007 Conference and Exhibition. Phoenix, AZ.

Workforce. (2012). "Survey: 45 Percent Would Cut Salary for Flexibility." Retrieved September 4, 2012 from www.workforce.com/article/20120830/NEWS01/120839992/survey-45-percent-would-cut-salary-for-flexibility#.

Worthman, C. (2006). *What's Your Story?* Chicago, IL: Kaplan Publishing.

Zachary, L. (2009). "Filling in the Blanks: Informal Mentoring Is About Being in the Right Place at the Right Time and Fostering Boundless Professional Support and Guidance Within Organizations." *T+D*. 63(5): 63-66.

——. (2011). "Mirror, Mirror: 6 Development Conversations to Have With Yourself." *T+D*. 65(5): 70-71.

Index

D

HOW TO PURCHASE ASTD PRESS PRODUCTS

All ASTD Press titles may be purchased through ASTD's online store at **www.store.astd.org**.

ASTD Press products are available worldwide through various outlets and booksellers. In the United States and Canada, individuals may also purchase titles (print or eBook) from:

Amazon– www.amazon.com (USA); www.amazon.com (CA)
Google Play– play.google.com/store
EBSCO– www.ebscohost.com/ebooks/home

Outside the United States, English-language ASTD Press titles may be purchased through distributors (divided geographically).

**United Kingdom, Continental Europe,
the Middle East, North Africa, Central Asia,
and Latin America:**
Eurospan Group
Phone: 44.1767.604.972
Fax: 44.1767.601.640
Email: eurospan@turpin-distribution.com
Web: www.eurospanbookstore.com
For a complete list of countries serviced via Eurospan please visit www.store.astd.org or email publications@astd.org.

South Africa:
Knowledge Resources
Phone: +27(11)880-8540
Fax: +27(11)880-8700/9829
Email: mail@knowres.co.za
Web: http://www.kr.co.za
For a complete list of countries serviced via Knowledge Resources please visit www.store.astd.org or email publications@astd.org.

Nigeria:
Paradise Bookshops
Phone: 08033075133
Email: paradisebookshops@gmail.com
Website: www.paradisebookshops.com

Asia:
Cengage Learning Asia Pte. Ltd.
Email: asia.info@cengage.com
Web: www.cengageasia.com
For a complete list of countries serviced via Cengage Learning please visit www.store.astd.org or email publications@astd.org.

India:
Cengage India Pvt. Ltd.
Phone: 011 43644 1111
Fax: 011 4364 1100
Email: asia.infoindia@cengage.com

For all other countries, customers may send their publication orders directly to ASTD. Please visit: **www.store.astd.org**.